INSIGHT

SeVILLe
CÓRDOBA & GRANADA

CHANNEL

APA PUBLICATIONS L

Part of the Langenscheidt Publishing Group

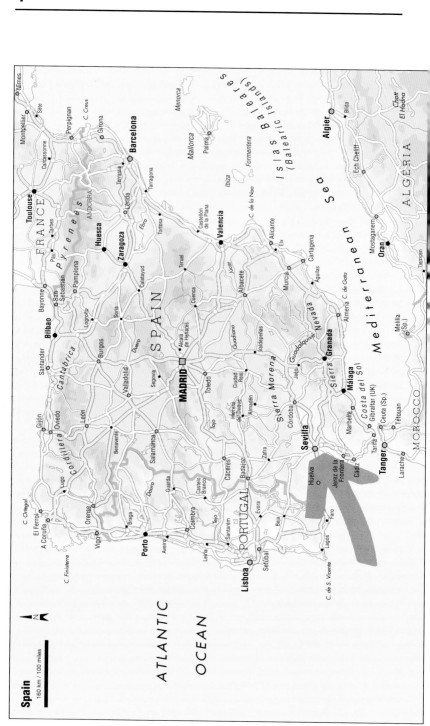

introduction

Welcome

This is one of 133 itinerary-based Pocket Guides produced by the editors of Insight Guides, whose books have set the standard for visual travel guides since 1970. With top-quality photography and authoritative recommendations, it brings you the very best of Southern Spain's three great cities, Seville, Córdoba and Granada, in a series of itineraries designed by Insight's specialist on the region. The tours cover all the highlights – Seville's Cathedral and Reales Alcazares, Córdoba's Mezquita and Granada's Alhambra – but they also explore the cities' old Jewish and Moorish quarters beyond the blockbuster sights, with frequent recommendations for shopping, lunch and *tapas* en route. In addition to the city tours there are three excursions into the countryside around the cities, to the Doñana National Park from Seville; to the Montilla and the Sierra Subbética from Córdoba; and into the Sierra Nevada and the Alpujarras from Granada. Supporting the itineraries are sections on history and culture, eating out, shopping and practical information, including a list of recommended hotels.

Nigel Tisdall first visited Andalusia in the mid-1980s, travelling there by train, in an old stiff-backed compartment decorated with lace curtains and table lamps. While researching this guide, he again took the train, but this time a Talgo, a sleek express complete with video screens. He describes Andalusia as one of the most exhilarating regions of Spain. 'It will always be a hotbed of Spanish cliché – the birthplace of flamenco, the cradle of bullfighting, a playground for gypsy passion, but it is brimming with energy, and Seville has become one of the most fashionable and hi-tech cities in southern Europe.'

This edition of the guide was expanded by the late **Mark Little**, who was a resident of the Costa del Sol and a regular contributor to Insight Guides, and updated by **Dorothy Stannard**, the Executive Editor in Insight Guides' London office.

LEISURE ACTIVITIES

CALENDAR OF EVENTS

PRACTICAL INFORMATION

MAPS

CREDITS AND INDEX

Pages 2–3: the Alhambra
Pages 8–9 Seville's Plaza de España

History & Culture

The history of the Río Guadalquivir, one of Spain's great rivers, reflects that of the south of the country. Now bloated with silt, it is a portly descendant of the fast-flowing, frequently flooding Baetis (Blessed) river that the Romans knew. From the mountains of northeastern Jaén, its waters wend their way westwards for some 600 km (375 miles), carving an ever-widening valley that culminates in Las Marismas. These broad marshlands stall its entry into the Atlantic beside the sherry town of Sanlúcar de Barrameda. When their fleets arrived here in the 1st century BC the Romans could sail upriver as far as Córdoba, a strategic point already colonised by Phoenician, Carthaginian and Iberian settlers.

Birthplace of Trajan and Hadrian

The Romans laid the ground plan of southern Spain, building roads, bridges and aqueducts. They established Córdoba, the home of Seneca and Lucan, as the capital of Hispania Ulterior, and redeveloped many of the prehistoric settlements built alongside the Baetis, including Hispalis (now Seville), Carmona and Itálica. The vicinity's numerous archaeological excavations have produced many an artefact that now graces the museums and stately homes of Seville and Córdoba. Of these the most famous is the gold jewellery that constitutes the Carambolo treasure in Seville's Museo Arqueológico. This incredible collection testifies to the wealth of the kingdom of Tartessus that flourished here in the 8th and 9th centuries BC. Near Santiponce (on what are now the western outskirts of Seville) you can wander amid the crumbling ruins of Roman Itálica, birthplace of the emperors Trajan and Hadrian, while at Carmona you can see the remains of the necropolis and amphitheatre.

The fall of the Roman Empire led to the rise of the Visigoths, who set up their capital in Toledo. A number of Visigoth fountains, arches and columns can still be seen lurking inside Andalusian monuments constructed many centuries later. In AD711 the Moors – principally Arabs and North African Berbers – landed at Tarifa. This arrival marked the start of a phenomenal advance: in seven years the Moors conquered virtually the whole peninsula. What had begun as a daring foray was to result in eight centuries of Moorish rule and the flowering of a great civilisation.

The Moors called their new land al-Andalus, and the river that fed it Guad-al-Quivir (Great River). By the 10th century, Córdoba, the capital of al-Andalus, had become the most important city in Europe. It was four times its present size, and had a university, libraries, public baths, workshops, street-lighting and more than 1,000 mosques.

Left: the richly decorated dome of Córdoba's La Mezquita
Right: a Tartessian mask dating back to the 8th or 9th century BC

The greatest of these, La Mezquita, still stands as a testimony to this golden age, which reached its apogee with the construction of the palaces at Medinat al-Zahra (now Medina Zahara, just outside Córdoba). Today their partly restored ruins barely hint at the opulence of a royal pleasure park that had its own zoo, mint, fabric factory and arsenal. At its centre stood a pool filled with mercury; when stirred, the sunlight's reflection would flash round the surrounding marble patios and the gold and silver tiles of the roofs.

Moors Bearing Gifts

Fabulous wealth grew from the Moors' talent for irrigation in the rich lands of the Guadalquivir Valley. The Greeks had introduced the vine and the olive – both cultivated intensively by the Romans – but it was the Arabs who added the orange and the almond tree, along with rice, aubergines, saffron, cotton, silk-farming, Merino sheep and herbs, spices and fruits. They also, like the Phoenicians before them and the British long after, exploited the mineral resources of the surrounding sierras.

Inevitably, it did not last. By the 11th century the refined glory of the Umayyad Caliphate had disintegrated into feuding *taifas* (factional kingdoms). These were easily overrun by the strict and austere Almoravids,

Christopher Columbus

In 1485 the Genoan-born Christopher Columbus (1451–1506) travelled to Iberia to elicit support for his 'Enterprise of the Indies' – a voyage intended to reach the shores of the East by sailing west across the Atlantic. Aged 34, Columbus (who may have been of Spanish-Jewish descent) was a widower with a five-year-old son, had prematurely white hair, and had already sailed to Madeira, Iceland and the Gold Coast.

After a rejection by the Portuguese court, he sought an audience with Fernando and Isabella. The commission they ordered to assess his proposals took four years to reach its verdict: 'vain and worthy of all rejection'. Columbus retreated to the monastery of La Rábida, near Huelva, but its prior, who had been Isabella's confessor, managed to get him recalled to the court.

Columbus sailed on 3 August 1492 from Palos de la Frontera (near Huelva) with three caravels, *Nina*, *Pinta* and *Santa María*. On 12 October they sighted land – a Bahama island – and a few hours later the Spanish flag was planted in the New World.

The great mariner made three further voyages. In 1493 he sailed from Cádiz and discovered Puerto Rico and Jamaica; in 1498 he sailed from Sanlúcar de Barrameda and reached the mouth of the Orinoco; in 1502, sailing from Seville, he discovered Panama. In the last years of his life he went to live in Santa María de las Cueva, a Carthusian monastery on the Isla Cartuja, Seville, where he wrote four autobiographical books, mourned the loss of his governorship over lands he had discovered, and hatched new plans, such as the liberation of Jerusalem. The restored monastery was the centrepoint of Expo '92 and is now a museum.

After Columbus died in Valladolid in 1506, his remains undertook a mysterious voyage of their own. In 1509 they were brought back to La Cartuja, but were exhumed again in 1536 and possibly transferred to Seville's cathedral. Around 1544 they were shipped to the Caribbean island of Santo Domingo (the Dominican Republic), but were later moved to Havana cathedral and purportedly returned to Seville cathedral in 1899. What ended up where is anybody's guess, but one thing is certain: an awful lot of places can stand up and say with all honesty 'Columbus was here'.

whose Berber armies were summoned to prevent a Christian reconquest. They were succeeded by the more liberal Almohads, who established their capital in Seville – the greatest of the *taifas* – and built the Giralda and the Torre del Oro, two of Seville's finest monuments.

The Decline of Al-Andalus

In 1212 the Christians defeated the Almohads at Las Navas de Tolosa in the Sierra Morena, a turning point in the 700-year *Reconquista*. By 1236, Fernando III had captured Córdoba, and in 1248 he took Seville. Fernando was aided by the complicity of the first Nasrid king, Ibn-al-Ahmar, who had retreated from Jaén to the mountains of the Sierra Nevada and a new power base in the former Almoravid capital of Granada. As a result of a peace treaty with the Christians, the kingdom of Granada – which covered the modern provinces of Málaga, Granada and Almería – survived as a vassal state for 250 years. The city flourished, not least on account of an influx of Muslim refugees and artisans from other captured cities. Indeed the newcomers played a key role in building the Alhambra, the Nasrid dynasty's memorial to the swansong days of Al-Andalus. At the same time the Christian king Pedro the Cruel employed Moorish craftsmen to build another tribute to this fading world – the Alcázar in Seville.

In 1492 the Catholic monarchs Fernando and Isabel captured Granada, Columbus discovered the New World, and the Jews were expelled from Spain. By then the notorious Inquisition had been in force for 12 years (it was to survive until 1821), *autos-da-fé* (burnings of heretics) were a fact of Sevillian life, and *conversos* (converted Jews) were having their wealth confiscated for investment in projects such as Columbus's second voyage. In 1503 the monopoly of trade with the New World was awarded to Seville's Casa de la Contratación, and the city prospered.

Above: life in Moorish Spain
Right: the Moors admit defeat

One of its employees, Amerigo Vespucci, gave his name to the new continent, Hernando Cortés sailed from Seville to ravage Mexico, and Fernando Magellan circumnavigated the globe. *Conquistadores* returned laden with gold and new curiosities such as peppers, tomatoes, quinine and tobacco.

By 1588 Seville had a population of at least 80,000, and a stature equal to that of Venice. But from the end of the 16th century it began on a slow, descent into decadence, a decline exacerbated by the expulsion of the *moriscos* (converted Moors) in 1610 and a terrible plague in 1649. During the 16th and 17th centuries Seville acted as a transit point for trade, administration and emigration. Its Lonja (Exchange), near the Cathedral, financed by a quarter-percent tax on the import of silver, is now the Archive of the Indies, where you can see the signatures of these early colonisers.

Church Wealth

These were heady days in Seville. Miguel de Cervantes (1547–1616), who served time in Seville's prison, recorded its colourful, roguish underworld in his novels; Bartolomé Esteban Murillo (1617–82) painted the beggars and other characters that filled the city's crowded streets. The Church, its coffers filled to bursting by the activities of the Inquisition, acquired a wealth that enabled it to build for itself luxurious city-centre sanctuaries that to this day force pedestrians into circumnavigatory detours. At one point the city had more than 70 convents. They were

Architectural Terms

Alcázar: Moorish palace
Alcazaba: Moorish castle
Aljibe: cistern
Artesonado: inlaid, coffered wooden ceiling, often with star-shaped patterns
Azulejo: coloured and patterned glazed ceramic tile
Mudéjar: work carried out by Moorish craftsmen under Christian rule
Mozarabic: work by Christian craftsmen under Moorish rule
Patio: inner courtyard
Plateresque: A Renaissance style characterised by richly ornamented surface decoration, similar to that wrought by a *platero* (silversmith).

richly decorated with paintings and sculpture by artists such as Velázquez, Cano, Zurbarán, Murillo and Leal – all members of what is now referred to as the Seville School. Their works can be seen in Seville's excellent Museo de Bellas Artes.

In 1717 the silting of the Guadalquivir forced the Casa de la Contratación to be moved south to Cádiz, thus hastening Seville's decline. Córdoba and Granada were now merely provincial backwaters in a demoralised country whose empire had been reduced by the 1701–14 War of the Spanish Succession. In the 18th and 19th centuries Andalusia gained a reputation as the home of gypsies, brigands, *majos* (dandies) and matadors that enchanted northern Europeans. Seville was seen as a city of aristocratic seducers called Don Juan and street-wise barbers called Figaro, while a sultry gypsy girl by the name of Carmen worked in the heat of its famous tobacco factory. In reality, however, Andalusia was a place of political chaos and deep poverty: by the beginning of the 19th century, 72 percent of the farming land in Seville was owned by an elite and invariably absentee landlord class that comprised barely five percent of its population.

Travellers and Romantics

Poverty contributed to the appeal of southern Spain for numerous aristocratic travellers who hired mules, boats and carriages to tour its provinces. They enjoyed its dilapidated state, exotic landscape and Moorish-Oriental heritage. The Alhambra – by now a picturesque ruin – inspired many a Romantic eulogy. Washington Irving swam in its ancient pools, Théophile Gautier cooled sherry in its fountains, and hotels appeared on the hill. But it was the passionate, sensual lifestyle of the Andalusians that really set northern hearts pumping. Hans Christian Andersen, visiting Andalusia in the 1860s, admitted his disappointment that he had experienced 'just a little encounter with bandits'. One intrepid lady traveller, en route to the Sahara in the same period, confessed that, after hearing a guitarist in Granada, 'you are ready to make love and war'.

Spain – which meant Andalusia to these visitors – was in vogue. This fashion was encouraged by the nation's victories in the Peninsular War (1809–14), its low cost of living and the growth of trade interests such as sherry. Granada and Seville topped the bill of places to see: 'Seville, the marvel of Andalusia, can be seen in a week' declared Richard Ford in his 1845 *Handbook for Spain*, a masterly work that did much to put Spain on the tourist map. Córdoba tended to receive, as it does today, a more perfunctory inspection.

By the end of the 19th century, Spain had lost virtually all of its remaining colonies, and it still lacked political stability. The nation remained neutral in World War I but in the 1920s it became bogged down in a war of independence with its one-time master, Morocco, the northern half of which had been a Spanish Protectorate. In an attempt to create a lasting order out of chaos, General Miguel Primo de Rivera assumed power in

Above Left: bust of Cano, an artist of the Seville School
Right: the legendary Carmen

a semi-dictatorship that had the concurrence of King Alfonso XIII: the pastiche pavilions built for the 1929 Ibero-American Exposition in Seville are a legacy of his period in power.

In the 1930s Ernest Hemingway wrote *Death in the Afternoon*, a paean to the 'noble art' of bullfighting, but it was fighting of a different nature that characterised that decade in Spain. Almost one million people were killed in the Spanish Civil War (1936–9), including many who were executed at the start of the conflict in Seville, Córdoba and Granada, which were among the first cities to be taken by Franco's Nationalist forces. One such victim was the Granada-born writer, Federico García Lorca. Indeed many artists, writers and intellectuals volunteered their support for the Republican cause, but they could not stand between Franco and a fascist victory.

In the aftermath of World War II, in which Spain remained neutral, the country was left isolated and impoverished. Franco's dictatorship lasted until his death in 1975, a period of steady economic advance scarred by political and cultural repression. Many Andalusians migrated to the northern industrial cities or abroad, leaving the countryside deserted. Franco's acceptance in 1953 of American military bases in exchange for loans, along with Spain's subsequent admission to the UN, accelerated its economic recovery and led to the development of mass tourism during the 1960s.

Post-Franco

In 1975, monarchy returned in the shape of King Juan Carlos, soon to be followed by democratic elections. In 1982 the Socialist PSOE party, led by the charismatic Sevillian lawyer Felipe González, won a sweeping victory that paved the way for long overdue investment in the region. The great manifestation of this was Expo '92 in Seville, which brought new roads, high-speed trains and a building boom to the regional capital.

And yet, for all the high-tech facelifts, the romantic, rose-in-the-teeth view of Andalusia persists. The Andalusians themselves foster this image in their patios, bars, *peñas* (clubs) and *ferias* (fairs). Andalusia will always be Spain spiced with the tang of North Africa, a mountain-locked land racked by summer heat and fed by the waters of the Guadalquivir.

Above: a traditional *tapas* bar in Seville

HISTORY HIGHLIGHTS

history/culture

circa **10000BC** Prehistoric settlers in Andalusia during Palaeolithic times, as evidenced by the cave paintings at La Pileta (near Ronda).

2000–500 BC The kingdom of Tartessus flourishes in the area around Seville.

1100BC The Phoenicians found Gadir (Cádiz).

3rd century BC Carthaginian forces conquer Andalusia.

218BC Roman colonisation of Spain begins with the Second Punic War.

1st century BC–3rd century AD The Romans further develop agriculture and construct roads and aqueducts. Itálica, Carmona and Seville are founded; Córdoba becomes the capital of Hispania Ulterior.

400–500 Domination by the Visigoths.

711 Moorish armies cross the Straits of Gibraltar; they conquer the peninsula within seven years.

756–1031 Umayyad dynasty rules over al-Andalus. Córdoba emerges as the capital of Muslim Spain; work starts on La Mezquita. In 929, Abd ar-Rahman III proclaims caliphate of Córdoba.

1086 The Almoravids, fundamentalist Muslim Berbers, invade Spain. They are expelled in 1147 by the Almohads, who build the Great Mosque of Seville.

1212 The Almohads are defeated at the Battle of Las Navas de Tolosa. By 1248, Fernando III takes Córdoba and Seville.

1237–1492 Nasrid dynasty rules the Kingdom of Granada. Construction of the Alhambra. In the 1360s Pedro the Cruel builds Seville's Alcázar; work starts on the cathedral in 1401.

1469 Marriage of Fernando V to Isabel I unites Aragón and Castile.

1492 Granada falls to Fernando and Isabel; Columbus discovers America.

1500s Seville granted trade monopoly with the New World, resulting in prosperity for the city. In the 1520s work begins on the cathedral in Córdoba's Mezquita, on Granada's cathedral, and on Charles V's palace in the Alhambra.

1600s The country's prosperity turns to decadence. Seville suffers a decline as the Guadalquivir silts up and trade moves to Cádiz.

1759–88 Carlos III introduces enlightened reforms.

1809–14 Peninsular War: all three cities are occupied by the French.

1800s Spain struggles to establish political stability and loses its colonies.

1929 Ibero-American Exposition held in Seville.

1936–9 Spanish Civil War: Seville, Córdoba and Granada are occupied by Franco's Nationalists, parts of eastern Andalusia are held by Republicans.

1975 Franco dies; Juan Carlos I becomes king.

1982 The country votes into office a socialist government led by Sevillian Felipe González. Andalusia is granted new autonomous powers.

1986 Spain becomes a member of the European Union (EU).

1992 Seville stages Expo '92. Celebrations mark the 500th anniversary of Columbus's discovery of America.

1996 José María Aznar's conservative Partido Popular replaces the socialists.

1999 Seville's Olympic Stadium, built for its failed bid to host the 2004 Olympics, opens.

2004 A month after devastating terrorist attacks in Madrid police foil an attempted attack on the high-speed rail link between Madrid and Seville. The socialists return to power, under José Luis Rodriguez Zapatero.

2005 Gay marriage is legalised in Spain, despite the protestations of, among others, the Roman Catholic Church.

2007 Trial of the Madrid train bombers.

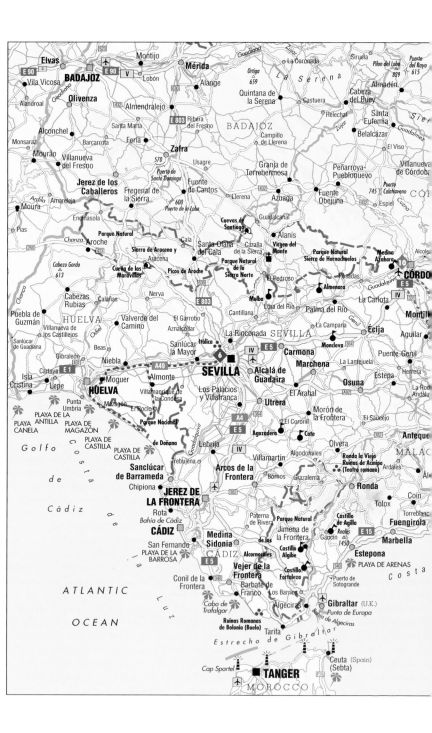

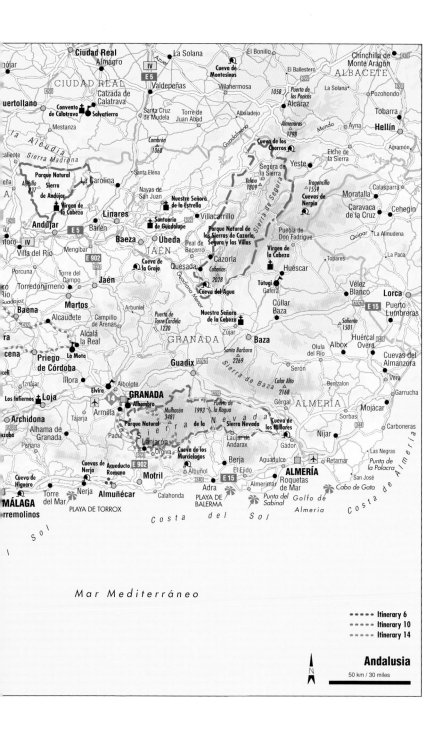

Andalusia

- - - - - Itinerary 6
- - - - - Itinerary 10
- - - - - Itinerary 14

50 km / 30 miles

Seville

L et's build a church,' said the architects of Seville cathedral, 'so big that we shall be held to be insane.' And they did – a vainglorious feat that squats in the city centre like an obstinate bag-lady. The cathedral, with its great Moorish tower, La Giralda, is Seville's best known landmark, and worth the climb if only to orientate yourself in the jumble of narrow streets.

Seville has had a long-standing love affair with the grandiose. Next to the cathedral is Pedro the Cruel's splendid Alcázar, inspired by the Alhambra and enlarged by Charles V. To the south, the immense tobacco factory is the second-largest building in Spain, after Felipe II's Escorial palace near Madrid. Beyond are the expansive remains of the pavilions, plazas and parks built for the 1929 Ibero-American Exposition.

The city also has a distinctive panache, most obvious in its intense celebration of Semana Santa (Holy Week) and the subsequent Feria (April Fair). The style and energy of the Sevillian character came to the fore when the city became an international stage for Expo '92. The legacy of this investment bonanza can be seen in new transport infrastructure (several new bridges, Santa Justa railway station and an expanded airport), a new theatre, restored museums and upgraded hotels. Further investments were made to back Seville's failed bid to host the 2004 Olympic Games, especially on the Isla de la Cartuja. Yet, in spite of the city's progressive outlook, it remains a quiet, intimate city that is sensual and faintly decadent.

Getting Around

Getting around the city is easy. The old town, which lies on the east bank of the Guadalquivir, can be crossed on foot in about 30–45 minutes. Puerta de la Macarena, the northern gate to the medieval city, and Plaza Nueva, near the centre, are two of the main bus terminals. In addition, the Sevilla Tour (a hop-on, hop-off open-top tourist bus) links the main sights. It can be joined at any point, but sets off from the Torre del Oro, as do a variety of river cruises. Horse-drawn carriages, a lovely way to visit the Plaza de España and the Parque de María Luisa, especially in the late afternoon and early evening, congregate around the cathedral and outside the Alfonso XIII Hotel, Puerta de Jerez. It is best to check the price before trotting off (the tourist office can advise on the approximate rate); be aware that prices soar during the April Feria.

On the western side of the Guadalquivir river lies Triana, an old working-class district with few sights but plenty of inexpensive bars, restaurants and street markets. In the evening it is worth strolling over the Puente de Isabel II to visit pleasant terrace tapas bars that line the promenade down to the Puente de San Telmo.

Left: the 600-year-old Cathedral Santa María de la Sede
Right: topping the Real Fábrica de Tabacos

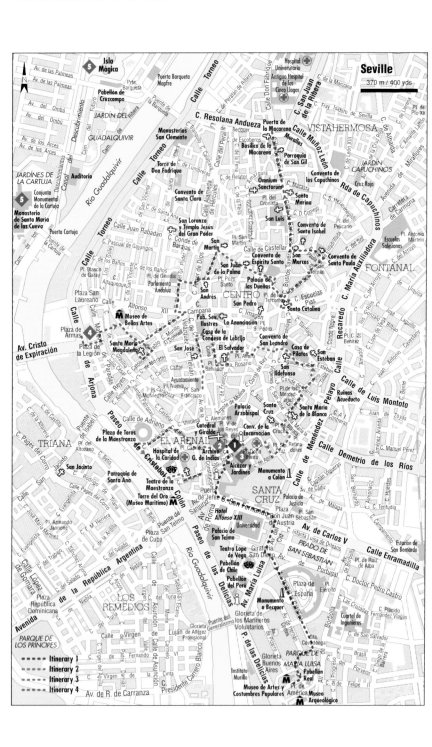

1. CATHEDRAL AND THE REALES ALCAZARES
(see maps, p22 & 25)

The first tour focuses on Seville's great monuments of the Islamic and Mudejar periods: the Cathedral with its Moorish minaret, and the Reales Alcazares, the palace built by the Almohad dynasty and later adapted and extended by Christian kings.

The cathedral and the Reales Alcázares are diagonally opposite one another on the Plaza del Triunfo. There is also a branch of the tourist office here. The cathedral is the best place to start, not least because it offers an overview of the city from its tower, but note that it doesn't open to tourists until 11am (worshippers can attend mass at 8.30am and 10am, and the prayer chapel is open from 8am). The Reales Alcázares opens at 10am; it is closed on Monday.

The **Cathedral Santa María de la Sede** (Mon–Sat 11am–5pm, Sun and holidays 2.30–6pm; admission charge, which includes ascent of the tower; concessions for senior citizens and students), dates from 1401 but occupies the site of a great mosque built by the Almohads in 1172. Its massive proportions reflect the Christian architects' desire to trump the grandeur of their Muslim predecessors. Of other cathedrals around the world, only St Paul's in London and St Peter's in Rome are larger. Roman pillars from Itálica surround it; the steps, **Las Gradas**, were for centuries Seville's main meeting-place.

As you approcah the cathedral, be sure to look up for a clear view of **La Giralda**, the tower of the Almohad mosque (now the cathedral's bell-tower.) built by Ahmed Ben Basso between 1184 and 1198 and one in a trio of similar minarets built by the Almohads (the other two being El Koutubia in Marrakesh and the Tour Hassan in Rabat). Notice the silhouette of its crowning weather-vane *(giraldillo),* and a revolving bronze statue that represents Faith. This is not the original 16th-century statue, but a more recent copy.

There are several entrances to the cathedral. The main one for independent visitors is the **Puerta de San Cristóbal** (groups enter via the Puerta del Lagarto). A reception area leads through a small museum, containing paintings (including work by Zurbarán and Murillo) and church plate, to the southwest side of the cathedral, with the shadowy depths of the cathedral's cavernous interior stretchingto the left. Straight Ahead is the **Coro** (choir) and **Capilla Mayor** (main chapel), which has a huge Gothic *retablo* depicting scenes from the Old and New Testaments, begun in 1482

Right: the Patio de los Naranjos

by the Flemish sculptor Pieter Dancar and not finished for a further 82 years. A mass of gold, it is one of the richest altarpieces in the world.

Turn right to inspect the **Tomb of Christopher Columbus**, supported by four pallbearers representing the kingdoms of Castile, León, Aragón and Navarre. Many of Columbus's voyages were planned in Seville, as is documented in the Archivo General de Indias *(see Itinerary 2, page 29)*. It is not certain that the elaborate sarcophagus contains the remains of the great discoverer, as Columbus's widow had these taken to Hispaniola in the Caribbean, from where they were later moved to Cuba and then back to Spain, a circuitous journey that was poorly documented. Attempts to test the DNA of the bone fragments have been inconclusive.

The **Capilla Real** (Royal Chapel) is reserved for worshippers. It is dedicated to the Virgen de los Reyes and contains a silver urn with the relics of

Fernando III, who expelled the Moors from Seville and Córdoba; nearby are the resting places of his wife Beatrice and son Alfonso X (the Wise).

La Giralda

On the northern side of the cathedral is the entrance to **La Giralda**, the original Moorish minaret which was capped with a Christian belfry, the ultimate *Reconquista* symbol. The tower is 97 metres (300 ft) high, including the weather vane, and the ascent (a gently rising ramp rather than stairs) provides a slide show of the city through the slender windows. Look out for some of the archaeological finds of the cathedral, displayed at points

Above: the Sacristía Mayor. **Left:** one of the 25 bells in La Giralda's belfry

along the ascent; they include a pair of 14th-century Mudejar doors combining Gothic motifs and verses from the Koran. You will emerge in the belfry, which offers panoramic views of white-washed houses and terracotta-tiled roofs, pierced only by the domes and bell-towers of the city's churches and convents, as well as the new-money monuments that have transformed the city more recently: to the west, beyond the bullring, are the bridges built for Expo 92 (including the wishbone arch of the Puente de la Barqueta); to the east is the modern railway station, Santa Justa.

Back at ground level, near the access point for La Giralda, is the **Puerta del Lagarto** (Gate of the Lizard), named after the life-sized wooden alligator that hangs from the ceiling), a replica of a real alligator given to Alfronso X by the Sultan of Egypt. This leads into the the **Patio de los Naranjos**, a courtyard lined with orange trees, a legacy of the original mosque and in the 16th century a sanctuary for criminals.

You can exit the cathedral from here, but if you have time it is well worth investigating the side chapels and Chapter House. Backtrack past the Columbus tomb to inspect a series of side rooms housing ecclesiastical treasures. Beyond the chapel of Los Dolores is the **Sacristía de los Cálices**: amongst its many works of art is a common anachronistic depiction – this one by Goya – of the Giralda with two 3rd-century Sevillian saints, Santa Justa and Santa Rufina, martyred during Diocletian's persecution of Christians. Next door is the **Sacristía Mayor** with more works by Zurbarán, Murillo and Van Dyck, along with some of the relics that are paraded through the streets during Semana Santa. Don't miss the keys given to Fernando III by the Muslim and Jewish communities following the reconquest of the city in 1248. In the southeast corner of the cathedral, a passage leads to the **Sala Capitular** (Chapter House), containing an *Immaculate Conception* by Murillo and a marble floor that mirrors the design of the domed ceiling.

Tapas Lunch

Afterwards, a possibility for lunch is the **Cervecería Giralda** (Calle Mateos Gago 1), a busy tapas bar across the Plaza Virgen de los Reyes. The day's *raciones* normally include Sevillian dishes such as *huevos a la flamenca* (eggs with ham and vegetables) and *cazuela Tio Pepe* (casserole cooked with sherry). If you arrive before 1.30pm you should get a table.

Los Reales Alcázares

Suitably fortified, you are now in a position to take on the **Reales Alcázares** (Royal Palaces, win-

Seville Cathedral

50 m / 55 yds

N

Calle Alemanes · Placentines

Puerta del Perdón

Patio de los Naranjos

El Sagrario

Puerta de la Concepción · Puerta del Lagarto

Plaza Virgen de los Reyes

exit

La Giralda

Avenida de la Constitución

Puerta del Bautismo

Puerta de Palos

Puerta de la Asunción · Coro

Capilla Mayor

Capilla Real

Puerta de la Natividad

Tomb of Christopher Columbus ★

Puerta de la Campanilla

Sala Capitular

Puerta de San Cristóbal

Sacristia de los Cálices · Sacristia Mayor

entrance

Plaza del Triunfo

ter: Tues–Sat 9.30am–6pm, Sun 9.30am–1.30pm; summer: Tues–Sat 9.30am–7pm, Sun 9.30am–5pm; closed Mon; admission charge; concessions for seniors and students; audioguide available), entered from the Plaza del Triunfo. The palace lies on the site of the Dar al-Imara (House of the Governor), built by the Arabs in the 10th century, and the 11th-century alacazar, which was extended by the Almohads in the 12th century, when it became the official residence of the Almohad monarchs. When Fernando II conquered the city in 1248, it became the residence of the kings of Castile.

The most interesting part of the palace that you see today was built by Pedro the Cruel. For a Castilian king (1350–69) with a reputation for barbaric behaviour (though he was also known as Pedro the Just), it is perhaps surprising to find such a fulsome homage to the refined abstraction of Islam. Pedro, who adopted Arab dress, employed Muslim master builders from Granada and Toledo, and filled his court with Moorish entertainers, exemplifies the paradoxical affection the Reconquest monarchs seem to have felt for the culture they destroyed. Unfortunately he had little time to enjoy his Alcázar – he was murdered three years after its completion.

Enter through the **Puerta de León**, near a section of castellated walls

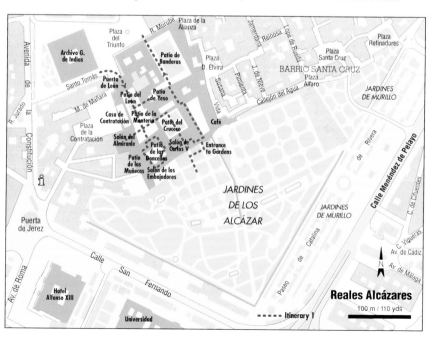

Reales Alcázares

100 m / 110 yds

- - - - Itinerary 1

that belonged to the original Almohad fortress. Inside, you will quickly discover that the palaces have undergone considerable renovations since the 14th century. However, first take the small flight of steps in the left-hand corner of the Patio del León to see the lovely Mudejar-style **Sala de Justicia** (Hall of Justice) and the **Patio del Yesio** (Courtyard of Plasterwork) that were part of the original 12th-century Almohad palace.

Regaining the Patio del León, proceed through the twin arches to the **Patio de la Montería**, a large courtyard added by Charles V. To the right is the **Casa de la Contratación**, a chamber of commerce created by Fernando and Isabel for the organisation of expeditions to the New World. Columbus was received here on his return from his second expedition. Inside you'll find the **Salón del Almirante** (Hall of the Admirals), with its 16th-century coffered ceiling, and a **chapel** containing the Virgen de los Navegantes.

Straight ahead on the Patio de la Montería rises the facade of Pedro's pleasure dome. Inside, bear left and pass through a vestibule to enter the opulent **Patio de las Doncellas** (Maids' Courtyard). The decoration was probably executed by craftsmen from Granada's Alhambra; Seville's Christian rulers allowed them to incorporate Koranic inscriptions (such as 'None but Allah conquers') into the intricate tiles and stucco work but had their own mottoes and coats of arms added. The upper storey is a 16th-century addition. The *azulejos* are the highlight of the impressive courtyard.

Straight ahead is the **Salón de Carlos V** with its fine coffered ceiling. To the right are three rooms that belonged to Pedro the Cruel's mistress, María de Padilla. Turn the corner for the **Salón de los Embajadores** (Ambassadors' Hall). The cedar cupola added in 1427 was embellished in subsequent centuries, but the room, with its triple arcade of horseshoe arches, remains resoundingly Moorish. Parallel to this room is Felipe II's dining room and bedroom.

Next is the **Patio de las Muñecas** (Dolls' Courtyard), named after a pair of tiny dolls' heads in the ornamentation on the columns, thought to have come from the palace of Medina Azahara in Córdoba. The upper floor is a mid-19th century 'enhancement'. To the left is Isabella the Catholic's bedroom, and ahead that of her only son, Don Juan. To the right is the **Salón de los Reyes Moros** (Hall of Moorish Kings).

Continue to the **Gothic Palace**. The **Banquet Room** was the setting for the marriage of Carlos V and Isabela of Portugal. Its large windows were installed by Felipe II; the Flemish tapestries depict his military campaigns in Tunisia in 1535. The apartments feature bright yellow *azulejos*, bursting with avaricious birds, snake-entwined cherubs and general Renaissance japery. The light-heartedness forms an ideal introduction to the Alcázar's gardens – a rambling paradise of box hedges and citrus groves punctuated with pools, pavilions and fountains. Look out for the entrance to the Baños de María de Padilla, the Moorish baths of Pedro the Cruel's mistress.

Above Left: the Reales Alcázares
Above Right: *azulejos* in the Gothic Palace

Take a Carriage to the Park

You may like to end the day by taking a carriage to the lovely Parque de María Luisa. You can travel there in style by horse and carriage – there are several *coches de caballos* ranks around the cathedral. To walk there, cross the Plaza del Triunfo, where a column celebrates the city's survival during the Lisbon earthquake of 1755, and turn left on the Avenida de la Constitución. This leads to the Puerta de Jerez, a veritable grand prix of traffic. Bear left around this roundabout to reach the **Hotel Alfonso XIII**. Opened in 1928, the hotel formed part of an ensemble of neo-Moorish, *azulejo*-covered buildings constructed for the 1929 exposition. Now in corporate hands (Best Western), the hotel has lost a little of its cachet, but it is well worth stopping to have a drink and nibbles around the fabulous grand patio, where a pianist plays in the early evening.

Continue along Calle San Fernando to the great hulk of the **Real Fábrica de Tabacos** (tobacco factory), completed in 1757, and now the science faculty of Seville's university. You can walk through the building: it still bears signs of the days when thousands of young *cigarerras* rolled cigars here. The factory girls piqued the interest of various foreign travellers, including Prosper Mérimée, whose story about one such girl inspired Bizet's opera *Carmen*.

Whether you walk through or round the building you will arrive at a junction with a statue of the *Reconquista* hero El Cid. Skirt round it, past the Teatro Lope de Vega and into the Avenida Isabel la Católica. The towers of the **Plaza de España**, inspired by the cathedral at Santiago de Compostela, will guide you. This semi-circular plaza with its splendid fountain and moat (currently drained during restoration) once housed the Spanish Pavilion. The *azulejo* panels below the colonnade depict aspects of the main cities and regions of Spain, running in alphabetical order from left to right.

Across from the plaza is the **Parque de María Luisa**, once part of the grounds of the baroque San Telmo Palace. A good way of exploring the

park is by bike (available to hire). There are two museums on the Plaza de América at the park's southern end: the **Museo de Artes y Costumbres Populares** (Tues 3–8pm, Wed–Sat 9am–8pm, Sun 9am–3pm; admission charge; free to EU passport holders) features costumes, decorative arts, and agricultural oddities; the **Museo Arqueológico** (Tues 3–8pm; Wed–Sat 9am–8pm, Sun 9am–3pm; admission charge; free to EU passport holders) covers neolithic to Moorish times and includes Roman finds from Itálica and Ecija. Don't miss the Carambolo Treasure, from the Tartessian culture.

When you are ready cut through to the Paseo de las Delicias, where you can hail a taxi or walk alongside the river, back to the city centre.

Above: the Plaza de España

2. EL ARENAL *(see maps, p22&26)*

Visit the New World records office, the bullring, the Arab Torre d'Oro on the riverside and the Hospital de la Caridad, a 17th-century hospital containing Murillo paintings and the finest baroque altarpiece in Spain

The centre of Seville is neatly divided by the Avenida de la Constitución. To the east is the cathedral and the Barrio Santa Cruz – the old Jewish quarter. To the west, on the other side of the avenue, lies El Arenal, a web of streets centring on Seville's bullring, La Maestranza.

Before exploring this area, you could visit the **Archivo General de Indias** (Mon–Fri 10am–1pm; admission free), in the heavyweight Lonja next to the cathedral. Formerly the stock exchange, the Lonja was designed in 1584 by Juan de Herrera, architect of El Escorial, the massive palace built for Felipe II near Madrid. Since the 1750s it has been a records office for documents relating to the discovery and colonisation of the New World. A small number of the millions of papers stored here are on permanent display in the exhibition rooms up the grand stairs, but you really need to speak Spanish to get the most out of a visit.

Nuns' Cakes

From the Lonja cross over Avenida de la Constitución and turn right then left into Calle Almirantazgo. An archway to the right of the café-restaurant La Amazara leads into the little-visited **Plaza del Cabildo**, the scene of a coin collectors' market on Sundays. Look for a small shop, El Torno (tel: 95 421 9190), selling cakes, biscuits and knitted babywear made by nuns from convents in and around Seville. Back on Calle Almirantazgo turn right through another arch, walk down Calle Arfe and turn left into Calle Antonia Díaz. The restaurants around this junction of streets are good dinner options: straight ahead is the Mesón Cinco Jotas and opposite a takeaway *freiduría* (fried

Above: La Maestranza, Seville's 18th-century bull-ring

fish shop – evenings only). Around the corner El Buzo and Bar Mesón Serranito serve Sevillian dishes in a bullfighters' ambience.

At the bottom of Calle Antonio Díaz is **La Maestranza** bullring (9.30am–7pm, closed from 3pm on fight days; admission charge), in the impressive **Plaza de Toros**. Built in 1760, La Maestranza is the second-oldest bull-ring (after Ronda) in Spain. Guided 20-minute tours (in English and Spanish) take in the bull-ring, museum, matadors' chapel, operating theatre and stables.

The Riverside

From La Maestranza, cross the road to the banks of the Río Guadalquivir, renamed the Canal de Alfonso XIII in 1948 when the river was diverted further west to prevent flooding. The river was re-opened for Expo '92, enabling visitors to cruise around the Isla de la Cartuja, the exhibition venue. Across the river to the north you'll see an iron bridge (built in 1852) crossing over to Triana, a blue-collar neighbourhood, where Seville's dockers and stevedores traditionally lived.

Turn left to walk down the pleasant Paseo de Cristóbal Colón. Ahead is the 13th-century **Torre del Oro**, constructed by the Almohads to anchor an enormous chain that stretched across the river as part of the city's fortifications. Today it features a small maritime museum (Tues–Fri 10am–2pm, Sat and Sun 11am–2pm; small admission charge; free Tues). Hop-on, hop-off bus tours of the city and cruises down the Guadalquivir leave from here.

Retrace your steps a few metres, cross the road and walk past the gardens of Seville's opera house, the **Teatro de La Maestranza** (Calle Nuñez de Balboa), which opened in 1991. At the end of the street is the **Hospital de la Caridad** (Mon–Sat 9am–1.30pm, 3.30–6.30pm, Sun 9am–1pm; admission charge; audiotours available), founded in 1674 and still functioning as a charity hospital. Its chapel, exemplifiying such institutions' great patronage of the arts during Seville's Golden Age, is lined with paintings representing death, the vanity of glory, the act of charity, and judgement, including ghoulish works by Valdés Leal (above the door and opposite) and several paintings by Murillo. The high altar is considered to be the finest baroque altarpiece in Spain.

Opposite the hospital, in a small garden, you will see a statue of Don Miguel de Mañara, the hospital's founder, who is considered to be the role model for Don Juan, the cynical lover who boasted of having 1,003 Spanish mistresses. The hospital became a point of call for Romantic writers

and artists who believed Seville to be the hotbed of the lascivious south. Byron explained why in his own *Don Juan*:

'What men call gallantry, and gods adultery,

Is much more common where the climate's sultry.'

Such matters might be discussed over a coffee in La Moneda café in the ramshackle **Real Casa de Moneda** (former royal mint and earmarked for restoration) round the corner on Calle Santander.

3. CITY WALK VIA CASA DE PILATOS *(see map, p22)*

An afternoon stroll through the pretty back streets of the Barrio Santa Cruz, visiting the Mudejar-style Casa de Pilatos and ending in the shops of Calle Sierpes. Start at about 4pm on a weekday to arrive in Sierpes when the 'paseo' is in full swing and its cafés are bubbling with life.

From the exit of the Reales Alcázares on Plaza del Triunfo, follow the general drift of people up Calle Gloria to enter the **Barrio Santa Cruz** (www.santacruz.com), the former Jewish quarter that was refurbished in the 1920s and has been metamorphosing into a picturesque tourist centre ever since. Continue up to Plaza de los Venerables and then to Plaza de Santa Cruz, framed by Sevillian mansions and with a 17th-century iron cross in the centre. Further on, Calle Mezquita takes you to the Plaza Refinadores (Polishers' Square).

Look for a small alley – Calle Mariscal – that will take you up to the Plaza de Cruces (Square of Crosses) and another square. At the top turn right into Calle Ximénez de Enciso, at the end of which turn left towards the Hotel Fernando III for Calle Cespedes. This road wends its way to Calle Levies, where you will be confronted by a huge red-brick building (once a noble house, then a convent and now a government building). Bear left into the Plaza de las Mercedarias, then take Calle Vidrio until it becomes pedestrianised, turning left (by No 25) into a tiny alley, the Calle Cristo del Buen Viaje. This delivers you to Calle San Esteban. Turn left towards the restful **Plaza de Pilatos**, where stands a statue of the great painter Zurbarán.

Arab Artistry, Italian Grace

The **Casa de Pilatos** (daily 9am–7pm; admission charge for ground floor, plus an additional charge for the upstairs rooms) is said to have been modelled on Pontius Pilate's house in Jerusalem by its creator, the Marquis of Tarifa. Completed in 1540, it is decorated in Mudéjar style but has none of the introversion and claustrophobia found in Pedro the Cruel's earlier Alcázar.

Left: the Torre del Oro. **Above:** a courtyard of the Casa de Pilatos

Spacious and eclectic in style, it is a delightul combination of Italianate grace and Arab artistry. You enter first through a Roman-style triumphal arch, crossing the *apeadero* (carriage yard) to its central patio where arcades of Moorish arches are echoed by Gothic arches on the floor above.

This courtyard contains exceptionally fine *azulejos*: puzzle-book patterns in brilliant colours. The Roman statuary was imported from Italy. Walk to the

right, through the Praetorian Chamber, with its fine coffered ceiling, to a small garden. Continuing around the patio in an anti-clockwise direction, you will encounter the chapel and Pilate's study, which open onto further gardens.

A monumental staircase in the corner of the main patio leads to the upper floor and a late Mudéjar cupola (1537). If you have paid the higher admission charge, you can take a rather abrupt guided tour (in English) of the upstairs apartments, containing art and furniture acquired over the centuries by the palace's aristocratic owners; parts of the house are still used for domestic purposes by the Medinaceli family.

Shops and Pastries

When you leave the Casa de Pilatos, turn right to walk past the Hostal Atenas (Calle Caballerizas) to reach the ochre facade of the baroque Iglesia de San Ildefonso. Directly opposite, a brown metal door leads into the **Monasterio San Leandro**, where you can buy – via a brass-studded revolving drum from 9am–1pm and 4.30–7pm – its famous *yemas (see 'Heavenly Sweets' in Eating Out, page 70)*.

Leave the adjacent plaza by the far corner, where Calle Boteros then Calle Odreros wind through to the **Plaza Alfalfa**, scene of a pet market on Sunday

Top: the Plateresque facade of the Ayuntamiento (Town Hall)
Above: a knife grinder offers a glimpse of old Seville

mornings. If you're peckish, Horno San Buenaventura is heaven for cake-lovers. From here follow Calle Alcaicería de la Loza (by the Carlos Antigüedades shop) into the city's main pedestrian shopping area. First is the **Plaza de Jesús de la Pasión**, devoted to wedding-dress shops, followed by the popular **Plaza del Salvador**, where the Bar Alicantina is famous for its seafood *tapas*. Between the two is the Church of El Salvador, where archaeological excavations are uncovering finds from the Roman Temple and early Christian, Visigoth and Mozarbic churches that preceded the 17th-century building.

The Plaza del Salvador sits halfway up a length of shopping streets running north–south. For a good circuit of the shops, walk up to the top of Calle de la Cuna, turn left and then return down the city's main strolling and spending artery, Calle Sierpes. While passing along Calle de la Cuna look out for the **Palacio de la Condesa de Lebrija** (at No 8; Mon–Fri 11am–1pm, 5–7pm, Sat 10am–1pm; admission charge), another Sevillian stately home with a grand patio and stunning mosaics from Itálica. At the top of Calle Sierpes, La Campana (No 1) is another great cake shop and always busy. At the southern end of the street is the **Plaza Nueva** and the old **Ayuntamiento** (Town Hall, 1564) with its Plateresque facade; beyond is the Avenida de la Constitución and the cathedral.

4. THE FINE ARTS MUSEUM AND A SELECTION OF CHURCHES *(see map p22)*

A long walk through the backstreets, taking in the Fine Arts Museum and a selection of churches, culminating in the Basilica de Macarena on the northern edge of the old town.

In the centre of the Plaza de Armas, the **Old Córdoba Railway Station** (1889) is a fine example of Sevillian architecture that served as a reference point for the future styles of regionalism and modernism. Having housed the Sevillian Pavilion in Expo '92, it is now a shopping centre, flanked by a rather ugly member of the NH Hoteles chain.

With the river at your back, walk away from the river to Calle Marqués de Paradas, cross the road and walk up Calle Pedro del Toro to the Plaza del Museo and the **Museo de Bellas Artes** (Tues 3–8pm; Wed–Sat 9am–8pm, Sun 9am–2pm; admission charge; free for EU passport holders), the city's Fine Arts Museum, housed in the former Convento de la Merced Calsada. The museum was inaugurated in 1841.

For years the museum was closed for restoration, the completion of which was hastened by Expo '92. Remodelled by Juan

Right: the Museo de Bellas Artes

de Oviedo y Banderas in 1612, the building has three colonnaded patios bordered by two floors of galleries of works from medieval times to the early 20th century, with emphasis on the Seville School's paintings, altarpieces and sculptures, commissioned by the city's convents, monasteries and hospitals. The main chapel's baroque ceiling is so gloriously coloured that it competes with the art below. Look for works by El Greco, Pacheco, Velázquez, Zurbarán, Valdés Leal and Murillo, whose swooning virgins wreathed in misty cherubs are typical of the Baroque Seville School. Also worth seeing are vistas of the Guadalquivir with steamships docked by the Torre del Oro and Gonzalo Bilbao's 1915 tribute to the tobacco factory workers: *Las Cigarerras*.

Shopping Centre

From the museum, walk east down Calle Baillén to the late 17th-century church of **Santa María Magdalena** with its colourful cupola. It contains a *Life of Dominic* by Zurbáran.

Retrace your steps up Calle Baillén to the junction with Calle San Eloy, where you might want to stop for a coffee at Cafe Zafiro on the small plaza here. Alternatively try El Patio San Eloy, an atmospheric bar on Calle San Eloy. Continuing to the end of San Eloy, turn left into the small garden square of Plaza del Duque de la Victoria, which has a low-key clothes market (Thur, Fri, Sat). Also here is a branch of El Corte Inglés department store. Leave the plaza with El Corte Inglés on your left and walk along Calle Jesús del Gran Poder, past the Plaza de la Concordia.

In front of the Farmacia Militar, turn right into Calle San Miguel then left when you reach Calle Amor de Dios, a veritable showcase of Sevillian urban architecture. Immediately turn right into **Calle San Andrés** and the small, mostly Gothic church of **San Andrés**. Leave by Calle Cervantes, passing under the ceramic 'street chapel' of Nuestro Padre Jesús del Gran Poder. Ahead is the 14th-century Gothic church of **San Martín**. Leave the Plaza San Martín by way of Calle Viriato. Some 100 metres/yds away is the Gothic-Mudéjar church of **San Juan de la Palma**, finished in 1788; notice the baroque bell tower and the unusual rectangular stained-glass window over the entrance. To the right is the Renaissance facade of an old seignorial house, which is now a shop.

From the plaza you can see the bell tower of the **Convento de Espíritu Santo**. Continue along the Calle San Juan de la Palma and follow the convent wall into Calle Dueñas until you reach the entrance to the **Palacio de las Dueñas**, a palace owned by the Duchess de Alba. It isn't open to visitors, but, if the gate is ajar, you may catch a glimpse of the garden.

Take Calle Doña Maria Coronel then the first left, Calle Gerona. If hungry, try the El Rinconcillo café (No 32) before reaching the Mudéjar doorway of the church of **Santa Catalina**. Inside, note the Portal Gótico, the Mudéjar details and the tower. Turn left towards the Plaza de los Terceros then keep right at the Libreria-Anticuaria Los Terceros. About 50 metres/yds further along on the right is the 17th-century church of **Los Terceros**. The colonial baroque door at the back of the church dates from the 18th century.

At the **Plaza de San Román** is another Gothic-Mudéjar church. Take the left side of the church along Calle de Enladrillada. At the beginning of a long white wall turn left into Calle Santa Paula. At the plaza beyond you will find the **Convento de Santa Paula**. If you arrive during the posted visiting hours, knock on the right hand door. A nun will show you around the museum and offer to sell you some home-made sweets and marmalades.

Leave the plaza by way of Calle Santa Paula (which becomes Calle Los Siete Dolores de Nuestra Señora). **Plaza Santa Isabel**, a good place from which to admire the Renaissance facade of the huge church of the **Convento de Santa Isabel** before visiting the smaller Church of **San Marcos** beside the square. The church tower was once a mosque minaret; the Mudéjar windows date back at least to the 14th century.

The Most Beloved Virgin

Facing the church's main door, turn left and follow Calle de San Luis. Soon you will see, on the left, the three doors of the **Iglesia de San Luis** (1699), one of the best examples of Sevillian baroque. Continuing along Calle de San Luis, pass the small church of **Santa Marina** to the right and the **Parroquia de Gil**, before arriving at the **Puerta de la Macarena**, the gate in the old Arab walls. Next to the gate, the **Basilica de la Macarena** was built in 1949 as a church-museum to house Seville's most beloved Virgin – **La Esperanza-Macarena**. For a small fee you can see the statue, which leaves its pedestal once a year in Holy Week to be paraded through the streets.

Across the road from the basilica is the delightfully old-fashioned **Bar Plata**. Around the corner from here is the massive **Hospital de las Cinco Llagas**, which is now home to the regional parliament.

Left: inside the Convento de Santa Paula
Above: one of the Church of San Marcos's Mudéjar windows

5. THE ISLA CARTUJA *(see map, p22)*

Isla Cartuja, was the main site for Expo '92, whose pavilions are now serving a variety of purposes, from industrial to educational. There are two attractions for visitors: a 14th-century monastery and a theme park.

In 1992 Seville hosted the World Fair, Expo '92. To facilitate such a prestigious event, the city had to undergo a thorough transformation and a whole new town of pavilions and exhibition spaces was built on a 182-

hectare (450-acre) site on the island of Cartuja. The event attracted more than 41 million visitors and placed Seville firmly on the international map. The city is still appreciating the side-effects of this grand project. Various innovative bridges were built to span the Guadalquivir, notably the wishbone-shaped Puente de la Barqueta and the harp-like Puente del Alamillo. The city also benefited from a revamped airport, a new railway station and new roads.

A number of Expo '92's bold, high-tech pavilions have survived on Cartuja. Some form part of a Science and Technology Park, while others are utilised by the city's university. The island's restored 14th-century **Monasterio de Santa María de la Cueva** Tues–Fri 10am–8pm, Sat 11am–8pm, Sun 10am–3pm; admission charge), which was used as the Royal Pavilion during Expo '92, was once a home from home for Christopher Columbus. The great explorer's grave was located here for a time. Between 1841 and 1980 the monastery housed the Pickman ceramics factory, which was known for its Cartuja porcelain. Part of the monastery now incorporates the **Centro Andaluz de Arte Contemporáneo**.

Isla Májica Theme Park

Further north along the banks of the Guadalquivir, some 34 hectares (85 acres) of the Cartuja island are given over to the delights of the **Isla Mágica** theme park (daily from 11am in summer, but more restricted opening the rest of the year, so check www.islamagica.es; best accessed from Puente de la Barqueta) centring on the artificial lake built for Expo '92. The theme is the conquest of the New World, with plenty of hair-raising white-knuckle rides.

Other attractions on the island include the **Auditorio de La Cartuja**, an open-air auditorium that seats 11,000 spectators for its occasional performances, and the **Teatro Central**, a modern theatre that stages plays, concerts and dances. The northern part of the island features the large, leafy **Parque El Alamillo**. Of more recent vintage, the 60,000-seat **Estadio Olímpico** was built as part of the city's unsuccessful bid to host the 2004 Olympic Games. The stadium served as the venue for the 1999 World Athletics Championships.

Above: thrills and spills abound at the Isla Mágica theme park
Right: church in the hamlet of El Rocío on the edge of the Doñana Park

Excursion

6. THE DONANA NATIONAL PARK *(see map p18–19)*

Spreading over 500sq km (190sq miles) at the mouth of the Guadalquivir, the Doñana National Park is one of Europe's great natural treasures. This excursion takes in the park tour, with stops at the wine-making town of Bollullos, the shrine of El Rocío, and the port from which Columbus launched his famous voyage of discovery to the New World.

This excursion can be easily travelled in a day, but, if you join the morning tour, the best option is to spend the previous night in El Rocío.

The **Doñana National Park** can be visited only on the official tour, in specially adapted four-wheel-drive vehicles. Departing from the park's main visitors centre in El Acebuche in Huelva province, the tour lasts four hours. There is one tour in the morning and another in the afternoon every day except Sunday during summer, and every day except Monday during the rest of the year. To book a place, contact the Cooperativa Marismas del Rocío (tel: 959 430 432). Winter and spring are the best times to visit; in summer, especially in years when there has been little rainfall, the marshes can dry up.

The Largest Winery

Take the E-1 motorway west towards Huelva. After 51km (30 miles) you reach the turning for **Bollullos Par del Condado**, the principal town in the Condado de Huelva wine-growing area, which produces crisp whites, nutty *olorosos* and *finos* – a sort of rustic sherry. You could stop at the Casa del Vino at the town entrance to sample the local brew. To visit the Bodegas Andrade, the town's largest private winery, call ahead (tel: 959 410 106).

Leave Bollullos on the A-483 road, which takes you past the farming town of Almonte to the hamlet of **El Rocío**, on the edge of the Doñana Park. For most of the year, the place seems eerily deserted, but for three days in

spring it becomes the spiritual centre of Andalusia. This is when approximately a million pilgrims congregate for the annual Romería del Rocío fiesta, arriving by car, bus or, more traditionally, in ox-drawn carriages, on horseback or even on foot. The centre of attention is a small image of the Virgin Mary that was discovered here by a hunter from Almonte 700 years ago. You can visit the shrine where the famous image is kept.

El Rocío is a good base from which you can branch out if you are spending the night. Stay at the hamlet's unpretentious and friendly Hotel Toruño (tel: 959 442 323), some of whose rooms overlook the Doñana marshes, or at the slightly more expensive Cortijo Los Mimbrales (tel: 959 442 237), which offers comfortable lodgings in the midst of a citrus farm 1km (1½ mile) south of El Rocío. Two kilometres (1¼ miles) south of El Rocío is the La Rocina visitors centre, where you can pick up maps and brochures. A detour of 5km (3 miles) takes you to the **Palacio de Acebrón**, an incongruous and sinister-looking neoclassical palace at the park's edge. From here, an interesting, shaded and easy hiking path runs alongside the Acebrón stream.

The Elusive Lynx

Back on the main road, continue south for another 12km (7 miles) to reach **El Acebuch**e, the park's central reception centre and tour starting point. The Doñana park is a vital refuge for countless birds that migrate between Europe and Africa each year; some species spend the winter here, others nest in the park's marshlands.

But the most emblematic denizen of the park is the extremely rare Spanish lynx, the most endangered animal species in Europe. These nocturnal, prowling felines inhabit the thick underbrush of the upper reaches of the park. Sighting the elusive lynx is a rare experience indeed, even for the naturalists who work here permanently. You are more likely to spot wild boar and deer.

The tour covers around 70km (40 miles) and, though it takes in only a fraction of the park, it is enough to give you a good idea of the various habitats that exist here. You will be driven along sandy white beaches pounded by the Atlantic surf as far as the mouth of the Guadalquivir, before plunging into the park's flat marshlands. Next you travel through forests of umbrella pines to reach a landscape of sand dunes. These shifting waves of sand, constantly, if imperceptibly, on the move, engulf copses of pine trees. As the sands move on, only the trees are left behind, like weird natural sculptures starkly silhouetted.

If you have time, you might want to extend your visit to the region to take in the towns that played a part

Left: the annual Romería del Rocío

in Columbus's historic voyage in 1492. Heading south from El Acebuche, skirting the ugly high-rise holiday resort of Matalascañas, the road travels through pine forests to reach Mazagón, a quiet seaside village with a fine *parador* (tel: 959 536 300).

La Rábida Monastery

After 11km (7 miles) you will find the 15th-century Franciscan monastery of **La Rábida**, where Columbus showed up in 1485 in search of refuge and a sympathetic ear for his proposal. This he found in the figure of Fray Juan Perez, the former confessor to the Spanish queen. Today the monastery – which features a Mudéjar-style inner courtyard, a 14th-century church and the Sala Capitular, where Columbus planned the final arrangements for his voyage – makes for an interesting visit, on a guided tour conducted by a monk.

On the coast not far from the monastery is the **Muelle de las Carabelas**, which is a reconstruction of a 15th-century port complete with full-scale replicas of the three ships, the *Niña*, the *Pinta* and the *Santa María*, that delivered Columbus and his crew to the New World.

In the neighbouring town of **Palos de la Frontera**, where Columbus signed up most of his crew, you can see La Fontanilla, the fountain from which the famous flotilla extracted enough water to last the long journey across the Atlantic. It was from Palos's port that the flotilla sailed down the Río Tinto river to the ocean just before sunrise on 3 August 1492. In the intervening centuries the river changed course and today the town is landlocked.

Return to Seville by an alternative route, rejoining the E-1 motorway 18km (11 miles) from the town, heading east. Seville is a further 80km (50 miles) away. On the way it is worth stopping at the medieval town of **Niebla**, 2km (1¼ mile) off the main road, whose fortifications are particularly impressive. Two kilometres (1¼ miles) of walls, with five fine gateways, encircle the old part of town. Within, you can visit the 15th-century Castillo de los Guzmán, before heading back to Seville.

Above: a section of the Doñana National Park

Córdoba

Córdoba hugs a lazy bend of the Guadalquivir at the southern foot of the Sierra Morena, 140km (87 miles) east of Seville. For a city with such a glorious past – it was the capital of Roman Spain and then later of al-Andalus – Córdoba is delightfully provincial. The city's enduring attraction is the vast, innovative mosque constructed by the Moors on the north bank of the river between the 8th and 11th centuries: La Mezquita – one of the wonders of the world. The city's old quarter spreads out around this landmark, a compact warren of whitewashed houses, winding alleys and flower-filled patios.

It is possible to visit Córdoba for the day from Seville (a 30-minute journey on the Seville–Madrid AVE train; longer on other types of train; the tourist office in Seville can supply timetables), but it is well worth staying a night or two here, and, if you are driving, also taking in Medinat Al-Zahra *(see page 49)* and the Sierra Subbética. Córdoba's old quarter has several small hotels and *pensiones*, as well as a comfortable member of the NH Amistad chain, converted from a cluster of old properties in the Judería. There are also options in the modern city beyond the old quarter *(see accommodation, page 86)*. If you are here in summer ask at the Tourist Office (Plaza de las Tendillas and Posada del Potro in Plaza del Potro) for information about the *Noches de Embrujo* ('Nights of Charm'), a long-running festival of evening cultural events such as flamenco, open-air cinema, jazz and guided walks by moonlight.

7. LA MEZQUITA *(see maps, p43 & 45)*

La Mezquita is best visited in the early evening, when the sun has warmed its ancient stones, and the school groups have gone home. Spend the morning either exploring the labyrinthine old quarter or visiting the Alcázar *(see Itinerary 8, page 47)*.

Allow two hours for a visit to the mosque, and bring a jacket because it tends to be very cool inside. Before you set out consider calling **El Caballo Rojo** *(Cardenal Herrero 28, tel: 957 475 375; £££) to book a table for dinner. This famous restaurant close to the mosque and specialises in* antigua cocina mozarabe – *traditional Córdoban dishes spiced and sweetened with Moorish flavours – such as* cordero al miel *(lamb in honey) and* revuelto siglio IX *(scrambled egg à la 11th century).*

Left: the Puente Romana from Torre de la Calahorra
Right: one of several doors to La Mezquita

La Mezquita (Mon–Sat 10am–7pm; Sun 9am–10.45am and 2–7pm; admission charge; audioguide available) is situated at the heart of the old town, a short walk north of the Puente Romana over the Guadalquivir river. It is accessed through the **Patio de los Naranjos**, which you can enter from Calle Cardenal Herrero or the northern ends of Calle Torrijos or Calle Magistral Gonzáles Francés. This enclosed garden, originally the courtyard of the mosque, is an ideal place in which to get your bearings and read up on the building's history; the ticket office is also here.

The Mezquita's Stone Magic

Palm trees, Arabian tents, Roman aqueducts, fans, acrobats on each other's shoulders ... theories abound as to what inspired the Mezquita's architects to create the innovative pillar-and-arch design that makes Córdoba's mosque such a thrill. What is clear is that they began with a pile of assorted columns and capitals gathered from the earlier Visigothic church and other plundered sources in the area around al-Andalus. The builders may also have kept one of the Visigothic church walls in place – a possible explanation for the Mezquita's great mystery: why does the *qibla* (prayer wall), which traditionally faces east to Mecca, actually face south?

These columns, all of which are of differing height and stone, were ingeniously incorporated into the building – sunk into the ground, raised up, inverted – and then topped by other columns. Two tiers of arches, constructed of red brick and white plaster, then bridged the gap between them – the higher arch supporting the roof, the lower strengthening the grid of columns. The result is apparently top-heavy, but when repeated row upon row, it creates a momentum and harmony that is ultimately spacious and agile. Later architects elaborated on this basic form by interlacing and polylobing (an effect resembling a bitemark) the arches. The result, built more than 1,000 years before Escher's visual conundrums and the world of computer graphics, is stone magic.

The History of the Mosque

Construction of La Mezquita began in AD785, two decades after Abd ar-Rahman I, founder of the Umayyad dynasty, declared himself emir of al-Andalus. Until then Córdoba's Moorish and Christian communities had shared the site's Visigothic church, San Vicente, which was partitioned into two parts. After purchasing the Christian half of the church, the Moors built a new mosque, using the old buildings materials. The original mosque occupied only a quarter of today's site.

Over the course of the next two centuries, as Córdoba's wealth and prestige grew, successive rulers enlarged and embellished the structure, extending the mosque east and as far south as the Guadalquivir allowed. In 1236, when Fernando III captured Córdoba, the Mezquita reverted to Christian ownership: Catholic chapels were built between the Roman and Visigothic pillars and many of the entrances were blocked.

In the 16th century an extravagant cathedral was erected here, to the dismay of Carlos V, who said: 'You have built here something you could have built anywhere, but you have destroyed what was unique in the world.' This was rather ironic given that Charles had made his own 'improvements' to both the Alhambra and Seville's Alcázar, and that it was Charles who sanctioned the work in the first place.

An appreciation of the Mezquita's former glory therefore requires some deft mental manoeuvres and the subtraction of the Christian appendages. First remove the closed arches along the mosque's northern wall, then open all the doors in the walls surrounding the patio. Now lose the 16th-century bell-tower encasing the original minaret, swap the

Above Right: Mezquita columns and arches

orange trees for olive trees, palms and cypresses, and lastly add a well and a waterwheel to the fountains.

In Arab cities a mosque is less a private religious compound than an integral part of the neighbourhood; it is a combination of thoroughfare, meeting place and, at the appointed hours, a place of communal prayer. The patio functioned as a courtyard for ritual ablution before prayer, the faithful being summoned by the call from its slender minaret. Its main entrance would have been the **Puerta del Perdón** adjacent to this tower, which lies parallel to the principal entrance to the mosque, the **Puerta de las Palmas** (next to the four naves with wooden lattices).

Both gates were redecorated in the Mudéjar style but Puerta de las Palmas is still flanked by two Roman columns and a plaque inscribed in Arabic. In the manner of an architect's sign, the plaque states that, in the Muslim year 346, Abd ar-Rahman commissioned Said ben-Ayub to build the mosque.

Entering La Mezquita

Today you enter the hall of the mosque through a small door on the patio's southeast corner. Before resuming this itinerary in the far corner to your right (by the wooden lattices), you will probably want to explore the mosque at your leisure for a little while.

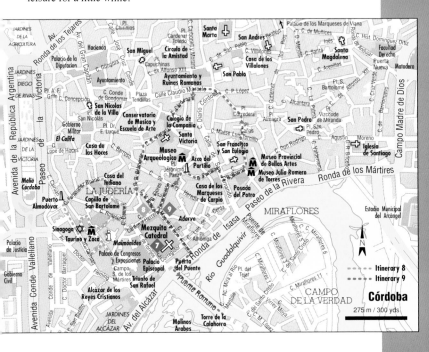

What little illumination there is shines above a lonely Visigothic font that, by the end of the day, is usually full of empty film canisters. This corner of the Mezquita is the original rectangle built by Abd ar-Rahman I. Along the walls, rows of Catholic chapels stretch into the gloom. Remove these and you can imagine how the serried pillars within the mosque formed a mesmerising continuation of the trees in the Patio de los Naranjos. This was part of a subtle transition from the mundane to the divine that culminates in the *mihrab*, the sacred niche in the prayer wall, where the Koran was kept.

Walking ahead in an anti-clockwise direction you will find yourself in the mosque's first extension, which was added by Abd ar-Rahman II in 833. (A slight ramp in the floor is evidence of the extension.) To the left is the rear of the cathedral *coro* (choir). Further on is the vaulted ceiling of an aborted church, planned in the 15th century. To the left you will see the domed **Capilla de Villaviciosa** where the old mosque's *mihrab* would have been. Through a cutaway you can see the **Capilla Real** next door, redecorated in the 14th century in Mudéjar stucco. This was the mosque's *maqsura* (royal enclosure).

Continuing ahead you enter the Mezquita's major enlargement, a legacy of the golden days of 10th-century Córdoba, constructed in 964 by al-Hakam II, son of the self-proclaimed Caliph Abd ar-Rahman III. He extended the southern wall right up to the river and built a new opulent *mihrab*, decorated with dazzling mosaics and a stunning star-ribbed dome that was subsequently copied throughout Spain. This lies beyond a set of railings – the bejewelled side-chambers formed Hakam's *maqsura*. Domed

Above: star-ribbed dome above the *mihrab*

skylights were introduced at this point on account of the considerable distance from the patio.

Turn left, pass the cathedral sacristy and enter the **third extension** of the Mezquita, built by al-Mansur in 990 to accommodate Córdoba's growing population. With the Alcázar to the west and the river to the south, his only option was to extend westwards, widening both the prayer hall and courtyard. Here the construction was conducted with more efficiency than artistry: the capitals of its uniform columns are less elaborate, the arches' red colouring is merely superficial paintwork. These aesthetic shortcomings are probably a reflection of al-Mansur's priorities, chief of which was the extension of his caliphate, which spread as far as Santiago da Compostela.

Beside you stands the towering Christian **Cathedral**. The construction of this stunning building began in 1523 and took two centuries to complete. With its narrow aisles and lofty **Capilla Mayor**, deliberately designed to humble worshippers and direct their eyes up towards the heavens, the cathedral stands in marked contrast to the Mezquita and its less hierarchical ethos. Among the cathedral's numerous fine features, a highlight is the carved mahogany choir stalls of the *coro* and the magnificent golden altarpiece containing 36 tableaux of the Life of Christ.

Returning to the outside world, take the western exit from the Patio de los Naranjos and walk south towards the river. Here you will pass the richest of the Mezquita's facades. The first doorway, St. Stephen's, was the original entrance to both the Visigothic church and Abd ar-Rahman I's mosque. Next you pass the extension by Abd ar-Rahman II and another door, St Michael's, which was a royal passageway from the Alcázar to the mosque's *maqsura*.

There are three other entrances to La Mezquita, all with brass-faced doors, that date to the al-Hakam II period. Look out for the central entrance which, with its Gothic arch stuck like a pointed hat on top of the Moorish horseshoe, neatly encapsulates the spirit of architectural oneupmanship that has created the Mezquita you see today.

To the River

For much of the day these edifices are spoilt by the noise, fumes and pollution of the local traffic. Once the Mezquita closes, however, the city suddenly relaxes. This is the ideal time for taking a stroll across the **Puente Romano**. Pause beside the silty waters of the Guadalquivir and, like so many before you, contemplate Córdoba in the fading light. Look out for the old Arab waterwheels, which are now very dilapidated, among the reed beds.

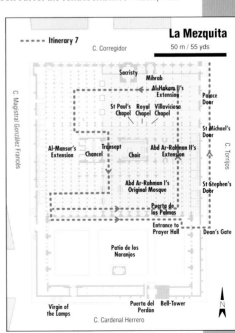

La Mezquita

- - - - Itinerary 7

50 m / 55 yds

C. Corregidor

Sacristy
Mihrab
Al-Hakam II's Extension
Palace Door
St Paul's Chapel / Royal Chapel / Villaviciosa Chapel
St Michael's Door
Al-Mansur's Extension
Transept Chancel
Choir
Abd Ar-Rahman II's Extension
C. Torrijos
Abd Ar-Rahman I's Original Mosque
St Stephen's Door
Puerta de las Palmas
Entrance to Prayer Hall
Dean's Gate
Patio de los Naranjos
C. Magistral González Francés
Virgin of the Lamps
Puerta del Perdón
Bell-Tower
N
C. Cardenal Herrero

córdoba itineraries

8. EXPLORING THE JUDERIA *(see map, p43)*

Córdoba's old Jewish quarter, the Judería, is situated to the northwest of the Mezquita, and can be explored in a couple of hours.

A Jewish community has resided in this quarter since Roman times. In the subsequent era, persecution by the Visigoths persuaded the Jews to side with the invading Moors. As a reward for their support, the Jews were permitted to remain in the city. For seven centuries they lived in generally fruitful coexistence with Córdoba's tolerant Muslim rulers, until Fernando and Isabel's edict of expulsion forced them out in 1492.

The quarter is now a relaxed maze of narrow streets, whose smarter residences and dilapidated historic buildings have been infiltrated by craft shops and souvenir stalls. Start in the **Calle Cardenal Herrero** and walk west towards a T-junction of streets that look like open markets. Take a sharp right down Calle Deanes, on which you should look out for No 16, which has a selection of the *filigrana de plata* (silver filigree) for which Córdoba has long been famous.

At the end of the street turn left into Calle Buen Pastor, which curls up to the Plaza Angel Torres. Nearby is the **Casa del Indiano**, a misleading name for a 15th-century Mudéjar-style gate. Walk past this to reach the **Puerta Almodóvar**, part of the Moorish city walls. If you turn left beyond this, you can follow the Rue de Kairouan, a pleasant, pool-lined promenade that runs beside the walls. At the end is a statue of Averroës, the 12th-century philosopher, medical writer and commentator on Aristotle, who was one of the most famous thinkers of Córdoba's golden age. Near here an arch in the walls readmits you to the Judería, just by the El Olivio restaurant.

A sinuous alley (Calle La Luna) leads to a crossroads at which you turn left on Calle Tomás Conde to reach the Plazuela Maimónides. Here the **Museo Municipal de Arte Taurino** (closed for renovation) is dedicated to the art of bullfighting. Continue up Calle Judios, past a statue of Maimónides, a Jewish philosopher whose 12th-century treatises on medicine were translated throughout medieval Europe. To your right you will find the entrance to the **Zoco**, a handicrafts market whose studios and workshops sell high-quality Córdoban leather goods, jewellery and ceramics.

The Synagogue

Further on, along Calle Judios, is the **synagogue** (Tues–Sat 10am–2pm and 3.30–5.30pm; Sun 10am–1.30pm; admission free) – one of three in Spain to survive the Inquisition (the other two are in Toledo). This remarkable and intimate place of worship dates from 1314 and has walls bearing Mudéjar ornamentation and Hebraic inscriptions. Over the centuries it has served as a hospital for rabies victims, a hermitage, a cobbler's, a school and a warehouse.

After touring the Judería, head back towards the river until you reach

Right: the 12th-century scholar Maimónides

Campo Santo de los Mártires square, one side of which is dominated by Córdoba's **Alcázar de los Reyes Cristianos** (summer: Tues–Sat 10am–2pm, 6–8pm; winter: 4.30–6.30pm; Sun 9.30am–2.30pm). The fortified palace was built by Moorish craftsman for King Alfonso II in the 14th century. The gardens are probably more interesting than the building itself.

When it comes to lunch, the Judería has plenty of options. Two of the best eateries are **El Churrasco** (Calle Romero 16, tel: 957 290 819) and **Taberna Pepe de la Judería** (Calle Romero 1, tel: 957 200744).

9. CITY WALK AND MUSEUMS *(see map, p43)*

This half-day itinerary takes you to the less-visited eastern part of Córdoba, where the traditional atmosphere of the old city intermingles with the modernity of the new. Afterwards try to make time to visit Madinat-Zahra, 8km (5 miles) west of Cordoba, though if you don't have your own transport you will need to go in the morning in order to catch the special daily bus *(see page 49)*.

Start in **Calle Cardenal Herrero** and walk east to its junction with Calle Magistral González Francés, at which you can walk up the narrow Calle Encarnación. **Taller Meryan** at No 12 is a workshop that sells a typical range of traditional Córdoban tooled and embossed leather goods. A quintessential part of Córdoba's character, which you will encounter frequently in this walk, is the patio. These inner courtyards were created by the Moors as cool central sanctuaries in which householders could escape the oppressive heat of summer. They often have a central fountain encircled by ferns, and surrounding walls bedecked with brightly flowering pot plants, patterned ceramic plates and colourful *azulejos*.

Turn right at the end, then left by the Hostal La Milagrosa (on Calle Horno del Cristo) into the **Plaza del Jerónimo Páez**. This square contains the province's **Museo Arqueólogico** (Tues 3–8pm; Wed–Sat 9am–8pm; Sun

Above: taking the weight off their feet in the old Jewish quarter

9am–3pm; free for EU passport-holders), housed in a Renaissance palace and currently being extended with a modern wing. Highlights include Roman mosaics and finds from Medina Azhara. La Cavea, a little café on the square here, is a good spot for a quiet coffee.

Take the pedestrian Calle Julio Romero de Torres, which winds round (past No 19) to descend the Calle del Portillo, where an ancient archway takes you beyond the old city walls – opposite this is the baroque Convento de San Francisco.

Turn right, cross the road, then take the second left to pass the Hostal Maestre (Calle Romero Barros), which finally delivers you into the attractive **Plaza del Potro**. The plaza gets its name from the *potro* (foal) that soars above its 16th-century fountain. A plaque on the wall of the museum *(see below)* reminds visitors that Cervantes mentioned the square 'en la mejor novela del mundo' ('in the best novel in the world'). The creator of *Don Quixote* stayed in the 13th-century Posado del Potro , now an arts centre (free entry), which functioned as an inn until the early 1970s. It contains a branch of the tourist office.

Fine Arts Museum

Also on the square is the **Museo Provincial de Bellas Artes** (Tues 2.30–8.30pm; Wed–Sat 9am–8.30pm; Sun 9am–2.30pm; free for EU passport holders), housed in the former Hospital de la Caridad. Its collection is largely based on works of art from disentailed monasteries and convents. They include works by the local master of the Baroque, Antonio del Castillo

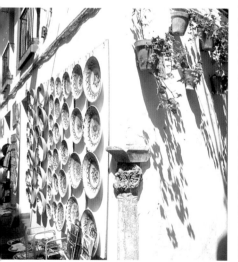

Saavedra and several works by the Seville artist Juan de Valdés. In the same building, the **Museo Julio Romero de Torres** is devoted to the works of a well-known local painter (1880–1930), who specialised in erotic portraits of sultry Andalusian women.

At the top (north end) of the Plaza del Potro, turn right and go down Calle Armas and Calle Sanchez Peña, to reach the large rectangular **Plaza de la Corredera**. Traditionally a site for the city's markets, bullfights and entertainment, the galleried brick buildings that enclose the square were built in 1688. Today it is the scene of an easy-going market selling clothes and household items.

Top: the foal that gives Plaza del Potro its name. **Left:** on the Calleja de las Flores
Right: enjoying the view from the Torre de la Calahorra

Exit the square via the northwest corner and walk down Calle R. Marín to the modern Ayuntamiento (Town Hall), which is flanked by a cluster of columns belonging to the remains of a Roman temple. If you want to visit the **Palacio de los Marqueses de Viana** (summer: 9am–2pm; winter: 10am–1pm, 4–6pm; Sun 10am–2pm; closed Wed and 1–15 June), a 10-minute walk north, turn right down Calle San Pablo to Plaza San Andres and then turn left *(see map)*. This is a 16th-century Córdoban stately home that was privately owned until 1980. It has an amazing 13 patios and 38 rooms and galleries crammed with antiques collected from all over the world. Whirlwind guided tours only.

Otherwise, from the Roman Temple continue uphill along Calle Claudio Marcelo, which culminates in Córdoba's bus-clogged central square, the **Plaza de las Tendillas**, from where Calle Jesus Maria and then Calle Angel de Saavedra and Calle Blanco Belmonte lead downhill towards La Mezquita, passing the music conservatory along the way. There is a good view of La Mezquita's tower from the Plaza Benavente. Take a small alley to the left of this plaza (past No 2) which leads to Calle Velazquez Bosco. This runs down to the Mezquita: on the way take a trip up the **Calleja de las Flores**, the vainest, most photographed street in Córdoba.

Circumvent the Mezquita, head for the Guadalquivir river and cross the Roman bridge to the **Torre de la Calahorra**. This 14th-century tower houses a museum devoted to life in Seville during its Moorish heyday (daily, summer: 10am–6pm; winter: 10am–2pm, 4.30–8.30pm). Exhibits include a model of the mosque as it was before the cathedral was built in its centre.

Medinat Al-Zahra

A fitting end to a view of Córdoba in Moorish times is an excursion by car, taxi or bus (bus leaves from Avenida Alcázar at 11am Tues–Fri, 10am and 11am Sat and Sun, site closed Mon) to the ruins of **Medinat Al-Zahra** (May–mid-Sep Tues–Sat 10am–8.30pm, until 6.30pm rest of the year, Sun 10am–2pm year round; free to EU passport holders), 8km (5 miles) west of the city on the A431. The remains of this once-fabulous palace-city illustrate the rise and fall of the Córdoba caliphate. In 1013, less than a century after Abd Al-Rahman III had ordered its construction, reputedly to please his Syrian wife, it was completely razed by rioting Berber soldiers.

Excursion

10. MONTILLA AND THE SIERRA SUBBÉTICA
(see map, p18–19)

Drive south from Córdoba into the heart of the Montilla region to sample rich Pedro Ximenez wines; cross the mountainous landscape of the Sierra Subbética nature park; return to Córdoba through olive country.

Take the NIV motorway west out of Córdoba, and turn off onto the N331 road, signposted Málaga. This takes you through rolling wheat and sunflower fields, past the castle towns of Fernán Nuñez and Montemayor. After 50km (30 miles) take the turnoff to **Montilla**, the main town in the region.

The principal grape here, the Pedro Ximénez, is said to be named after a German soldier in the Spanish imperial army, Peter Siemens, who brought the original cuttings from the Rhine in the 17th century). It is exceptionally sweet by nature, and its sugar content is further increased by spreading the harvested grapes on mats to roast in the sun. After crushing, fermentation transforms the sugars into alcohol, resulting in wines with a kick of 15–18 percent. Similar to sherry, they range from the crisp, dry and pale fino, to nutty, amber oloroso and amontillado, and velvety Dulce Pedro Ximénez.

Life in Montilla revolves around the wineries, the oldest and most famous of which is Bodegas Alvear, which dates back to 1729. You can visit the cellars of the huge winery complex in the centre of town, where the wine slowly matures in row upon row of ancient oak casks, each holding 500 litres. To visit, tel: 957 664 014.

Head south from Montilla to **Aguilar de la Frontera** and another fine bodega. The small **Toro Albalá winery** (tel. 957 660 046) produces some of the best aged sweet Pedro Ximenez wines in Spain. It also has a curious museum devoted

to old farming artefacts and wine-making paraphernalia.

For ornithologists, a short detour from Aguilar de la Frontera takes you to the lagoon of **Zoñar**, where you can spot various aquatic bird species, including the rare white-headed duck. A marked path around the lagoon starts from the visitors centre on the road between Aguilar and Puerto Alegre.

Back on the main N331 highway, 20km (12 miles) south from Aguilar is **Lucena**, which has a thriving furniture industry. Its large factories and showrooms attract buyers from Córdoba, Sevilla, Granada and the Costa del Sol. Pass this sector to reach the historical centre of Lucena, and one of the region's finest baroque churches, San Mateo.

From Lucena, take the A316 to **Cabra**, the entry point for the Sierra Subbética nature park. The A340 road to Priego de Córdoba takes you through spectacular scenery. For a sweeping view of the region, take a detour to the 1,200-metre (3,940-ft) Ermita de Nuestra Señora de la Sierra shrine.

180-jet Fountain

Priego de Córdoba, 30km (18 miles) from Cabra, is a veritable treasure trove of baroque art and architecture, and its churches, especially La Asunción, San Pedro and La Aurora, are well worth visiting. Also check out the colourful displays of geraniums along the old quarter's narrow streets at the foot of the castle. Finally, before you leave, see the enormous, 180-jet Fuente del Rey (King's Fountain) near the entrance to the leafy Priego park.

Head east from Priego on the A340 to the small town of **Almedinilla**, whose fascinating ruins of a large Roman villa are one of the best preserved of their kind in Spain. The ruins are covered by a protective iron roof. Press on eastwards to reach the N432 highway at **Alcalá la Real**, a town overlooked by La Mota castle. Like other castles in the region, it is evidence of the historical period when these towns guarded the frontier between Christian Spain and the Moorish kingdom of Granada.

Heading north back towards Córdoba, leave the mountains behind and plunge into a boundless landscape of neat rows of olive trees. Some of the finest olive oil in the world is produced in this part of Spain; one of the best-known producers is to be found in **Baena**, 50km (30 miles) from Alcalá la Real. The Nuñez del Prado family has been making *aceite de oliva* for seven generations. You can visit their olive mill, part of which dates from the 18th century, on weekdays; it is situated next to Baena's town park at Calle Cervantes 14.

Leaving Baena and heading north back to Córdoba, pass Espejo and, as a parting shot, yet another picture-perfect castle, this one dating from the 14th century. From here, it is 23km (14 miles) back to Córdoba.

Left: sampling the local wine
Above: an olive farmer poses

excursion from córdoba

Granada

O nly 80km (50 miles) from the Mediterranean coast, Granada stands a cool 685 metres (2,250ft) above sea level. Once based around three foothills of the **Sierra Nevada** – Albaicín, Sacromonte and Alhambra – the city now oozes out over the eastern end of the *vega*, the long fertile plain that, in Moorish times, was a vast market garden of orchards, farms and watermills. Further east the snowy peaks of the Sierra Nevada provide the waters for the city's two principal rivers, the Darro and the Genil.

11. The Alhambra
(see maps, p55 & 56)

Spend a day exploring the Alhambra hill, visiting the Alcazaba fortress, the Generalife gardens, Charles V's Palace and the Nasrid Palaces.

The highlight of any visit to southern Spain has to be the **Alhambra**, the palace-fortress of the Nasrid dynasty, the last rulers of Moorish Spain (Nov–Feb Mon–Sun 8.30am–6pm and Fri, Sat 8–9.30pm; Mar–Oct Mon–Sun 8.30am–8pm, Tues–Sat 10–11.30pm; admission charge, senior citizens from the EU are entitled to a reduction on production of their passport; free for under-8s; www.alhambra.org).

Visitors to the Alhambra are restricted to 7,700 per day. Tickets, which have three parts (the Alcazaba, the Generalife and the Nasrid Palaces, the latter can only be entered during the half-hour slot shown on the ticket) sell out quickly. To avoid the possibility of disappointment (especially in summer), it is best to book in advance from Banco Bilbao Vizcaya Argentaria (BBVA); tel: 902 224 4 60 (from Spain) or 34 91 537 9178 (from abroad) or buy direct from BBVA banks in Spain. You can book online at www.alhambratickets. com. To buy tickets on the day, arrive early or opt for a late afternoon visit.

A special minibus to the Alhambra leaves every 15 minutes or so from the Plaza Nueva, where you will also find taxis, but the traditional approach to the Alhambra involves a steep, half-hour walk up from the Plaza Nueva into the cool woods of the Alhambra hill, passing through the **Puerta de las Granadas** (Gate of the Pomegranates – the city's emblem) and then, by taking the left-hand route, following the inner walls. Among the gates and towers that you pass,

Left: the Alhambra's Patio de los Leones
Right: Puerta de las Granadas

A Brief History of the Alhambra

Construction of the Alhambra began in 1238 under the aegis of Ibn-al-Ahmar, who was the founder of the Nasrid dynasty. Ibn-al-Ahmar rebuilt the ancient fortress of the Alcazaba, originally separated from the main hill by a ravine (now the Plaza de los Aljibes) and diverted the waters of the Darro to supply the new citadel. Most of the palatial splendour you see today dates from the 14th century and was the work of Muslim craftsmen who fled here as al-Andalus fell to the forces of the Reconquest.

The Catholic monarchs Fernando and Isabel conquered the Alhambra, the last bastion of Muslim Spain, in 1492. They restored parts of the palaces, though the cathedral they installed in the mosque was replaced in the late 16th century by the Iglesia de Santa María. Ferdinand and Isabella also built the Franciscan convent (now the Parador).

Their grandson, Charles V, who demolished more than he replaced, built his palace on the site of the cemetery. With the expulsion of the Moors, several minor earthquakes and a gunpowder explosion in 1590, the Alhambra fell into decline.

Some 200 years later the Alhambra was ransacked by Napoleon's troops. They left it in a parlous state of decay which, ironically, is what endeared the Alhambra to the Romantic writers, artists and travellers then discovering (or inventing) the exotic Spain of the 19th century. 'The Alhambra', Benjamin Disraeli declared in 1830, 'is the most imaginative, the most delicate and fantastic creation that ever sprang up on a Summer night in a fairy tale.' Such eulogistic appreciation goes a long way to explaining why so many tourists gather here today.

By 1870 the Alhambra had been declared a national monument and today it is a UNESCO World Heritage site. You may want to read Washington Irving's *Tales of the Alhambra*, which is on sale in numerous shops in the area. The writer, an American diplomat, lived here for a few months in 1829.

look out for the **Torre de la Justicia**, surmounted by two Islamic symbols – a hand representing the faith's five tenets (the oneness of the deity, prayer, fasting, alms-giving and pilgrimage) and a key, representing the prophet's power to open and close the gates of heaven. You can enter the Alhambra at several points (you do not pay to enter the walled area itself, only the palaces, museums and gardens), but the ticket office for these is near the top of the hill, just below the car parks.

Your ticket will specify the half-hour in which you can enter the Nasrid Palaces, and this will determine the order in which you visit the other main components of the site: the Alcazaba (fortress) and the Generalife (summer palace). The latter is some distance from the rest of the site and takes at least an hour to visit, so is best left until last if possible. The itinerary outlined here heads first to the Alcazaba (visiting Charles V's Palace en route), then the Nasrid Palaces and then the Generalife.

Charles V's Palace

From the entrance, the route to the Alcazaba leads down through the Medina, comprising the homes, baths and workshops of the ordinary people living in the palace complex. On the way it passes the luxury **Parador de San Francisco**, a former convent dating from 1495, whose terrace-bar, with views over the Generalife, is a nice spot for a morning coffee (or evening drink).

Above Right: the Torre del Homenaje (Homage Tower)

Eventually the route reaches **Charles V's Palace** (Palacio de Carlos V). Commissioned in 1526 but built almost a century later and therefore never lived in by Charles, it displays a haughty, Renaissance grandeur that contrasts strongly with the intense, decorative detail of the Nasrid Palaces. The only surviving work of the architect Pedro Machuca, its power lies in the simplicity of the concept – a circle in a square, executed in unadorned stonework.

Part of the palace contains the **Museo de la Alhambra** (Tues–Sat 9am–2.30pm; free admission), containing items found at the Alhambra, Córdoba and Medinat Al-Zahra. The collection has many relics from the Alhambra's glory days: ceramics, *azulejos*, pottery lamps, carved roofbeams, marquetry chess boards, a copper minaret – all of which bring this great Moorish stage set to life. Look out for the lovely Jarrón de la Alhambra, a 14th-century Nasrid vase decorated with gazelles. The **Museo Bellas Artes** (Tues 2.30–8pm; Wed–Sat 9am–8pm; Sun 9am–2.30pm; free admission) occupies the upper floor of the palace. Push on through its worthy collection of religious paintings and sculptures and you will find in the 19th-century galleries a display of Romantic Andalusian art featuring coy and picaresque characters.

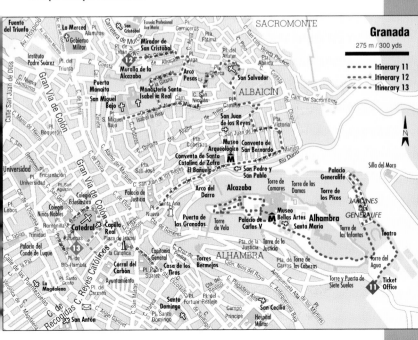

The Alcazaba

Now continue through the **Puerta del Vino** towards the battlements of the Alcazaba. This is the oldest part of the fortress – some sections date from the 9th century but the two towers overlooking the Plaza de los Aljibes (Square of the Cisterns) date from the 13th century. The Alhambra began life as a military garrison: the plaza was once a moat, then an underground cistern. A small kiosk here sells beers, soft drinks and *bocadillos*, and there are benches in the shade.

Enter the **Alcazaba** by the Torre Quebrada (Broken Tower) and wander around the Torre del Homenaje (Homage Tower) to reach the Plaza de Armas – which in former times was full of houses and barracks. Today only the dungeons and cisterns are visible. On its far side signs guide you towards the main tower, the **Torre de Vela** (Watchtower), the highest point of the Alhambra. En route you might enjoy the little-visited 17th-century **Jardín de los Adarves,** with its terrace offering classic views of the Sierra Nevada. There are yet lovelier views from the top of the Torre de Vela: for centuries the bell in the top of the tower was used to tell the farmers of the *vega* when to irrigate their crops.

The Alhambra's one-way system directs you down to the battlements and beyond, to the Machuca Gardens. The entrance to the **Nasrid Palaces** is close by.

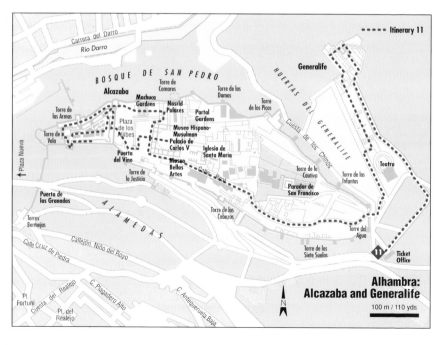

The Nasrid Palaces

The Nasrid Palaces constitute the inner sanctum of the Alhambra. The entrance is at the far side of Charles V's Palace. The first room, the **Mexuar**, was originally an audience chamber used for judicial and administrative business, though converted into a chapel in the 18th century. The *azulejos* are from Seville, and in Moorish times there would have been a cupola and lantern rather than the carved, wooden roof. At the end is the **Oratory**, from which there is the first of many fine views out over the Albaicín and Sacromonte hills.

Next along the tour is the **Golden Room** (Cuarto Dorado), another reception room, which was decorated in Mudéjar style after the Reconquest. Opposite is the **Mexuar Patio** and the facade of the **Comares Palace**. Here you can examine the intricate patterns of the plasterwork, in low relief, which was used extensively in the Alhambra. Islam proscribes the depiction of the human form and the Alhambra's craftsmen vigorously pursued the abstract. Their intention was to direct the eye to the infinite and concentrate the mind on the divine by a rhythmic repetition of floral shapes, interlocking geometric forms, multi-centred grids, and ribbons of Koranic inscription joined to proclaim the oneness of God. Such intricate decoration is often hidden behind bland exteriors and concealed entrances.

Take the short, narrow passage leading into the **Court of the Myrtles** (Patio de los Arrayanes, but also known as Patio de Comares), where another principle of Islamic architecture becomes apparent – the incorporation of natural elements, particularly light and water, as an integral and active part of the architecture. Now you are in the Serallo, the heart of the royal palace where foreign emissaries were received.

Walk around the long fish pond in a clockwise direction, passing a small niche that allows close inspection of the stuccowork. The faded colours in its recesses are a reminder that such ornamentation was once painted and gilded.
Adjoining the Court of the Myrtles is the
Barca Gallery, an antechamber to the
splendid **Comares Hall** (also known as
the Sala de los Embajadores/Hall of the
Ambassadors) where the Moorish kings
presided. Its impressive domed ceiling of
inlaid wood depicts the seven heavens
revolving around the seat of God.

Back at the Court of the Myrtles a
short passage leads into the harem, the
private section of the palace and the last
to be built. It is heralded by the **Court
of the Lions** (Patio de los Leones), said
to be the architectural swansong of a
doomed monarchy. Its design symbolises
the Islamic paradise: an enclosed garden (substitute plants for what is now
gravel) with a central fountain from which

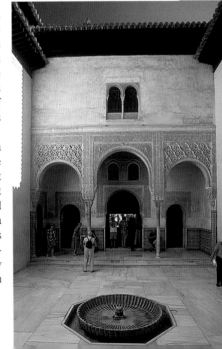

Above Left: the Patio de los Leones, Nasrid Palace. **Right:** the Nasrid Palace

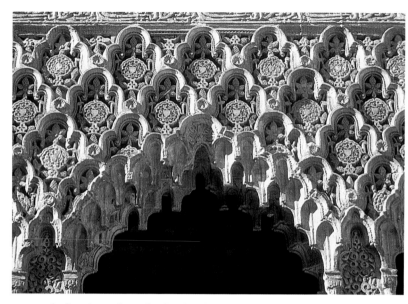

the four rivers of paradise flow into four restful pavilions surrounded by a forest of marble palms. Around the fountain stand 12 lions (gradually being restored), whose significance is not clear: they might represent the signs of the zodiac, or possibly the tribes of Israel.

The sultan and his entourage resided here, and in the adjacent four rooms: to the left as you enter are his wife's apartments, the **Hall of the Two Sisters** (Sala de las Dos Hermanas), which has a cupola said to be decorated with more than 5,000 cavities. Opposite this is the **Hall of the Abencerrajes**, used for entertainments; notice the beautiful octagonal ceiling. It was here that Abu el-Hassan (ruler of Granada 1464–1485) had the Abencerraje family murdered following the discovery of an illicit affair between his favourite concubine Zoraya and a member of the family. Ahead is the **Hall of the Kings** (Sala de los Reyes), behind which are some alcoves that were once bedchambers. The ceilings above are covered in leather and painted with scenes of courtly life, pre-

sumably by a Christian artist commissioned by the Moors.

Exit the patio through the Hall of the Two Sisters and you will come to the **Baño de Comares** (Royal Baths). The tiled chambers and fine, star-spangled domed roofs constitute one of the most evocative parts of the complex. You can wander down the terraces to the secluded corner of the Alhambra in which the 19th-century

Above: Nasrid Palace stucco
Left: Court of the Myrtles

American author Washington Irving lived in 'delicious thraldom' while writing his bestseller *Tales of the Alhambra*. The Lindaraja and Daxara Gardens were both apartments of the harem that were remodelled in the 16th century.

The exit from the palaces near the Torre de las Damas (Ladies Tower) leads to the **Partal Gardens**, or Western Gardens, which served as the servants' quarters and vegetable plots. You will pass a pavilion built above the fortress walls that faces a pool guarded by two lion statues, said to have come from a lunatic asylum that occupied part of the Alhambra during the mid-19th century. Nearby is a small Moorish oratory. On the other side of the gardens is **La Rauda**, a royal cemetery built by Mohammed I.

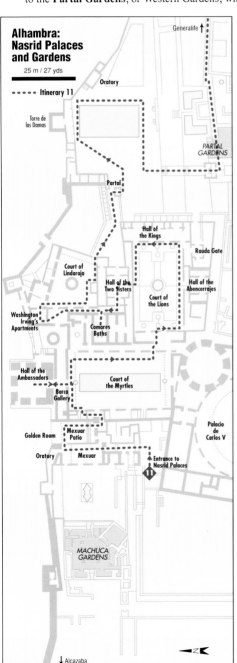

**Alhambra:
Nasrid Palaces
and Gardens**

25 m / 27 yds

- - - - **Itinerary 11**

Generalife

Oratory

Torre de
las Damas

PARTAL
GARDENS

Partal

Hall of
the Kings

Rauda Gate

Court of
Lindaraja

Hall of the
Two Sisters

Hall of the
Abencerrajes

Court
of the Lions

Washington
Irving's
Apartments

Comares
Baths

Hall of the
Ambassadors

Court of
the Myrtles

Barca
Gallery

Golden Room

Mexuar
Patio

Palacio
de
Carlos V

Oratory

Mexuar

Entrance to
Nasrid Palaces

11

MACHUCA
GARDENS

N

↓ Alcazaba

The Generalife

The Generalife (a name believed to derive from the Arabic *Gennet al-Arif* ("architect's garden") are widely considered to be the finest in all Spain, although the Italianate layout of the present gardens owes little to their Moorish origins. The fine arrangement of terraces, fountains, miradors and courtyards delights visitors at every turn. Among the highlights look out for the **Patio de la Acequia**, with its long, narrow pool flanked by water spouts, and the **Patio de los Cipreses** (Courtyard of the Cypresses), where the dead trunk of an ancient cypress tree is said to have marked the site of illicit assignations between Zoraya, a concubine of Abu

el-Hassan, and her Abencerraje lover, leading to the murder of the Abencerraje family in the Hall of the Abencerrajes *(see page 58)*.

Also, don't miss the **Escalera de Agua**, the stairway to the top miradors, whose bannisters carry water down the hill.

Also on the Alhambra Hill

Before leaving the Alhambra Hill (or perhaps revisiting it later during your stay), you may want to take in two attractions on the south side of the hill. The **Alhambra Palace** hotel (Calle Peña Partida), is a neo-Moorish fantasy, whose terrace has a great view of the city and the *vega* beyond and even as far as the Sierra Nevada. The great musician Manuel de Falla enjoyed a similar view from his home opposite the hotel. Born in Cádiz, the composer of *Nights in the Gardens of Spain* spent many years in Granada, where he was a friend and mentor of the poet Federico García Lorca. His home between 1922 and 1939, the **Casa Manuel de Falla** (Tues–Sat 10.am–2pm; admission charge; www.museo manueldefalla.com), a classic Granada house, has been converted into a museum that celebrates his life and works.

12. EXPLORING THE ALBAICÍN *(see map, p55)*

Piled up on a steep hill facing the Alhambra, the Albaicín was the heart of Moorish Granada and the seat of the royal court for two centuries before the Nasrids built their palaces on the opposite side of the Darro river. Its pretty streets and houses retain a Moorish flavour.

When the city fell to Fernando and Isabel in 1492 the Albaicín had 60,000 inhabitants; by the early years of the 17th century the persecution and expulsion of the rebellious 'moriscos' (Muslims who converted to Christianity) had reduced this figure to 6,000. Traditionally a poor quarter, the Albaicín now constitutes a pleasant maze of narrow streets lined with whitewashed houses, palaces surrounded by high walls, and churches and convents that have fallen into neglect. However, for all the signs of gentrification that seep through the Albaicín's many alleys and thoroughfares, its Moorish character persists.

This walking tour begins at the top of the Albaicín, and meanders down to the Darro river, which separates the Albaicín and Alhambra hills. You can climb up to the start from the **Plaza Nueva**, but you may prefer to take a mini-bus up to the **Mirador de San Cristóbal** from the Gran Vía. Mini-buses from the Plaza Nueva go as far as the Mirador San Nicolás *(see page 61).*

Top: the Patio de la Acequia in the Generalife
Right: Plaza Larga, the Albaicín

From the Mirador de San Cristóbal there is an excellent view over Granada and the *vega*: in the foreground you will see the old city walls of the Albaicín. From here you can take Calle Brujones (to the left of Tablao Flamcenco restaurant) and turn right to descend Cuesta de San Cristóbal.

Drop down the hill into the Plaza Almona, then turn leftwards to ascend into the **Plaza Larga**. This is the hub of the Albaicín – in the morning it hosts a bustling market, for the rest of the day it is an open-air café and meeting place. In the right-hand corner of the plaza stands the 11th-century **Puerta Nueva**, which has a defensive dog-leg passage. Having passed through the gateway, continue straight through the Placeta de las Minas, then turn right into Calle Aljibe de la Gitana. After a turn to the left you arrive at the small park – the Placeta del Cristo de las Azucenas. This adjoins two of the Albaicín's most famous buildings – the Moorish palace of **Dar al-Horra** and the **Monasterio Santa Isabel la Real**, which dates back to 1501.

A Postcard-Perfect View of the Alhambra

Here you are confronted by a choice: you can either turn right towards the palace or continue down the slope and turn right on Calle Isabel la Real, which leads to the monastery. In both cases the route leads to the tranquil **Plaza San Miguel Bajo**, which is a good place at which to stop for a drink or a light lunch. Note Bar Lara, which specialises in meats from the Alpujarras. From the plaza return along Cale Santa Isabelle la Real, which eventually turns into Camino Nuevo de San Nicolás, where a curve to the left will lead you up some steps to the Mirador de San Nicolás and a postcard-perfect view of the Alhambra.

Descend the steps and turn left to reach a small plaza that sits discreetly beside the Iglesia del San Salvador. Look straight ahead and you will be able to see the old city walls that run across Sacromonte hill, along with the abandoned caves that once formed Granada's old gypsy quarter.

From here you can zig-zag your way downhill by any of a number of routes that keep you facing the Alhambra. Several restaurants have sprouted

up along this walk, some offering patrons the relatively rare opportunity
to enter a flower-filled *cármen*.

Café Society

Probably the easiest route down from here is via Calle Placeta de Toqueros,
from which you turn left then right to descend the gentle gradient of the
Cuesta de la Victoria. Now you will find youself beside the Darro ravine. The
plaza here has a gentle, neighbourhood atmosphere during the day and is well
worth returning to in the evening, when it takes on a relatively cosmopolitan
atmosphere and is peopled by café-society dawdlers, basketball players and
baked-potato sellers. A range of bars along the **Paseo del Padre Manjón**
serve *tapas* and small dishes; La Fuente is the place to hear good-quality
Spanish pop music.

From here you can follow the Darro back towards the city centre. Several old properties along this route have been converted into interesting
hotels *(see Accommodation, page 87)* and there are a number of low-key bars.
On the way you will pass the Casa del Castril, home of the **Museo Arqueológico** (Tues–Sat 9am–8.30pm; Sun 9am–2.30pm; free for EU passport-
holders), and **El Bañuelo** (No 31, Tues–Sat 10am–2pm; admission free),
which houses well-preserved 11th-century Arab public baths with domed
roofs and star and octagon shaped vents. If you fancy a relaxing steam and
aromatherapy massage in a modern-day version of an Arab bath, there are
two possibilities. Close by, across the little bridge over the Darro and left
up Calle Santa Anna, past the tourist office, are the **Hammam Baños Arabes**
(tel: 958 229978), and at 41 San Miguel Alta, south of the Cathedral, is
Aljibe Baños Arabes (tel: 958 522867; www.aljibesanmiguel.es).

13. THE CATHEDRAL QUARTER *(see map, p55)*

The cathedral, built on the site of a mosque in 1523, is hemmed in by
buildings below the Gran Vía de Colón. This district of pedestrian shopping streets and leafy plazas is liveliest in the mornings.

Start with a coffe at one of the ring-side cafés of the bustling **Plaza de Bib-Rambla**, just west of Calle Reyes Católicos. Calle Pescadería leads to the **Mercado
Municipal de San Agustin** markets. From the centre of Calle Pescadería take
Calle Marqués de Gerona to the Plaza de las Pasiegas. Here you see the main
facade of the **cathedral** (Mon–Sat 10.45am–1.30pm, 4–8pm; Sun 4–7pm;
admission charge), designed in 1667 by Alonso Cano and considered to be one of the finest Renaissance facades in Spain.
Turn left and follow the walls of the cathedral around to Gran Via
and the main entrance for visitors. The cavernous
white interior, completed in 1714, is austere,
though the double organ is of interest, as are
the collection of illustrated manuscripts and
a series of rather gloomy paintings by
Alonso Cano, who was a painter and
sculptor as well as an architect.

Left: the Plaza Isabel la Católica statue

The Capilla Real and La Madraza

The most interesting part of the cathedral is the adjoining **Capilla Real** (10.30am–1pm, 4–7pm; Sun 11am–1pm and 4–7pm; admission charge; separate entrance on Calle Oficios, running alonside the Cathedral), the resting place of Ferdinand and Isabella, who commissioned this mausoleum. The marble effigies of Fernando and Isabel are upstaged by the larger ones of Felipe I and Juana de Castilla, which were placed there by their son, Carlos I (Charles V). The actual remains of the monarchs are in simple lead coffins in the crypt below the mausoleum. The chapel also contains a good little museum containing vestments, paintings, altarpieces, as well as Isabel's crown and sceptre.

Also on Calle Oficios is the site of Granada's Arab university, **La Madraza**, founded in 1349 by Yussuf I and now part of Granada University. If the door is open (restoration is in progress) you can inspect a small, richly decorated oratory across the patio. Carry on down the street and through a small gate and then turn left to enter the Alcaicería, a 19th-century reconstruction of the Arab silk market that originally stood here. Today it is a parade of souvenir stalls. Continue straight on and cross Calle Zacatin, a long pedestrian shopping street, to reach Calle Reyes Católicos. Directly across the road in Calle Lopez Rubio you will see the arch above the entrance to the **Corral del Carbón**, a 14th-century caravanserai that quartered travelling merchants and their pack animals. The interior courtyard, surrounded by three-storeyed galleries, hosts the regional tourist office.

For lunch, go back to Calle Reyes Católicos and turn right for the **Plaza Isabel la Católica**. The statue commemorates Queen Isabel's support for Columbus. From here you can take Calle Pavaneras to the small car-cluttered **Plaza Padre Suarez**, where **Seis Peniques** offers a range of set menus in an alfresco setting opposite the Casa de los Tiros, an early 16th century mansion. For a classier venue, you may want to try the cellar-restaurant at the bottom of this plaza, **La Alacena** (Tel: 958 221 105).

Above: the tombs of Fernando and Isabel in the Capilla Real

Excursion

14. SIERRA NEVADA AND THE ALPUJARRAS
(see map, p18–19)

To the Veleta peak in Sierra Nevada; then back down the mountain to explore the Alpujarra region on the southern slopes of the sierra, taking in the villages of Capileira, Bubión, Pampaneira and Trevelez.

Sierra Nevada's Mulhacen is, at 3,500 metres (11,500ft), the highest peak in Iberia. The snow-capped summit of the Sierra, providing a dramatic backdrop to the Alhambra, forms the classic postcard image of Granada. In 2000 Sierra Nevada and the surrounding 214,000 acres were declared a national park. It is also home to Spain's southernmost winter resort: between December and April it has 60km (40 miles) of marked ski slopes at altitudes ranging from 2,100 metres to 3,273 metres (6,900ft-10,750ft).

Much of the mountain is above the tree line, so the scenery is on the stark side when there's no snow, but the combination of high altitude and southern sun supports 4,000 plant species, along with ibex, eagles and an impressive range of butterflies. Hiking, horseriding and paragliding are among the activities on offer in the warmer months.

Europe's Highest Road
In the early years of the 20th century, diehard Granada skiers would lug their skis by mule-back over winding trails to reach the Sierra Nevada slopes.

These days a modern road takes you there in just over half an hour. This, the highest road in Europe, is popular with car manufacturers who want to test new models at high altitudes.

Halfway up the mountain is the El Dornajo Park visitors centre, where you can pick up maps and literature on Sierra Nevada's wildlife and outdoors activities. Further on is the main ski station, Pradollano. This was built with little concern for its aesthetic integration with the landscape, and it remains an ugly mixture of faux-Andalusian buildings, Swiss chalets and faceless concrete blocks. Unless you have business here (such as skiing) it is best to press on to the Veleta, the second-highest peak in the Sierra at 3,470 metres (11,380ft). The

Left: Capileira and Bubión

road ends within close range of the peak. If it's scenery rather than skiing that you are after, the best time to come is just before or after the ski season, when there is a bit of snow at the top of the mountain.

Pass of the Moor's Sigh

The most spectacular scenery is to be found on the southern slopes of the Sierra, the region known as the Alpujarra. You cannot drive across the top of the mountain to get there (the dirt road is off limits to visitors), so backtrack, towards Granada. Skirt the city, following signs to Motril, on the N323 road. A few miles from Granada is the Suspiro del Moro, (Pass of the Moor's Sigh). The name is a reference to Boabdil, the last Moorish king of Granada, who, heading for exile, paused here for a final, tearful look at the city he had lost to Ferdinand and Isabella. His mother retorted: "Weep like a woman for the city you didn't defend like a man".

Some 37km (23 miles) south of Granada is the turnoff to the town of **Lanjarón**. Due to several natural springs fed by the Sierra's melting snow, Lanjarón is famous for its mineral-rich water, which is sold all over Spain. And thousands of visitors "take the cure" at the town's *Balneario* (spa).

The town of **Órgiva**, 9km (5 miles) east of Lanjarón, marks the gateway to the Alpujarras region. Just before the town, take a left fork to the **Barranco de Poqueira**, the heart of the Alpujarra. Clinging to the valley sides are the villages of Capileira, at the top, Bubión in the middle, and Pampaneira at the bottom. **Bubión** is the region's tourism centre – here you'll find hotels, restaurants, crafts shops and other indications that the area is no longer Spain's best-kept travel secret. **Capileira** is quieter, **Pampaneira** the most pristine. In Pampaneira you will see the distinctive flat slate roofs of the local architecture, and the postage-stamp farms on terraces carved out of the hillside, alternating with rushing streams and chestnut forests.

Continuing your explorations of the Alpujarra, head eastwards from Pampeneira towards Trevelez. The route takes you through increasingly luxuriant, unspoiled scenery, past the small villages of Pitres, Pórtugos and Busquístar. It then climbs towards Trevelez which, at 1,476 metres (4,842ft), is the highest village in the country. **Trevelez** is famous throughout the country for its serrano hams, which are naturally cured in the crisp mountain air. But don't expect to spot any pigs here. The basic ingredient of serrano hams - pork shoulders and hams - are shipped in from elsewhere to hang in the dozen or so curing cellars at the bottom of the village, where they acquire their distinctive flavour and the privilege of being called Jamón de Trevelez. You can order this ham in any bar in Granada, but somehow it tastes much better up here, on the slopes of Sierra Nevada.

You can return to Granada the way you came or take a longer route, through somewhat bleaker mountain scenery, heading south and east from Trevelez to Torvizcón, then rejoining the original route at Órgiva.

Above: Jamón de Trevelez, a local speciality

ZAPATOS
DE
BAILE
PROFESIONAL

Botos de
VALVERDE

Calzados MAYO

ZAPATOS DE BAILE

Leisure Activities

SHOPPING

Mass-manufactured Andalusian mementoes include gypsy costumes, pairs of castanets, personalised bullfighting posters, mantillas, Mezquita wine-flasks and Alhambra table-lamps. Beyond these clichés, specialist shops sell quality hats, fans, handmade shawls, guitars and wrought ironwork *(esparto)*.

Leather goods, jewellery and ceramics are widely sold – keep an eye out for good-value shoes, silver filigree, decorative plates and bowls, *azulejos* and kitchenware. Cheap belts, wallets, bags and baskets are sold by African hawkers, who will barter.

If you're searching for gifts, consider sherry, convent-made sweets, olive oil, cassettes of guitar music, figs, honey, almonds and saffron. Other favourite Spanish purchases are *cava* (sparkling wine – try the Delapierre or Freixenet labels), cigars from the Canary Islands or Cuba, carved olivewood utensils, terracotta kitchenware, *paella* dishes, candle-holders, *sangría* jugs, Lladró porcelain, *alfombras* (carpets and rugs) and *jarapas* (cotton rugs and car-seat covers).

Seville

The main shopping street in Seville is the **Calle Sierpes**. This is the place for fashionable clothes as well as more *típico* fare, from fans to ceramics. Martian (No 48) offers a pleasing display of Sevillian ceramics and pottery. Zadi (No 48) has a serious collection of fans, mantillas and Lladró porcelain, while the old-fashioned Marquedano (No 40) stocks a classic range of Andalusian hats.

To the east, the Plaza de Jesús de la Pasión is the city's matrimony corner, with several jewellery shops. Beyond the northern end of Calle Sierpes you come to the Plaza del Duque de la Victoria, with Spain's largest department store, El Corte Inglés. Around the corner on Calle Alfonso XII Sevilla Rock sells Spanish pop and guitar music including flamenco and *sevillanas*.

For ceramics, La Alacena (further down Alfonso XII, at No 25) has top-of-the-range china and crockery from La Cartuja factory (now on the Carretera de Mérida). Puerta Triana (corner of Calle Santas Patronas and Calle Reyes Católicos) has a less expensive selection of painted plates, bowls and jugs while across the bridge in Triana, Cerámica Santa Ana (Calle San Jorge 31) is a rambling showroom-cum-pottery with both antique and modern *azulejos*.

On the east side of the Maestranza bullring, Jamón Real I – Esther Fernández Fdez. (Calle López de Arenas 5) sells Extremaduran wines, meats and cheeses, marmalade and home-made wines and liqueurs (it also has a small bar where you can sample products); there's another branch, Jamón Real II, at Calle Pastor y Landero 2.

Being a university town, Seville has many good book shops. One of the best is Vértice, across from the Old Tobacco Factory on Calle San Fernando.

Left: shoe shops abound
Right: the ultimate frilly dress

Córdoba

The English word 'cordwainer' is derived from Córdoba and testifies to the city's long tradition of high quality leather-work. In the area bordering La Mezquita you'll find studios and cobblers' workshops, such as the one at Calle Magistral González Francés 7 which specialises in riding boots.

Silver filigree (*filigrana de plata*) is also common. Look out also for two distinctive types of ceramic plate: the green and white Caliphal pottery based on 10th-century Arab designs, and the dark-green pottery from Lucena. Montilla wines and anis-flavoured *licor* from Rute are other specialities.

In the small shops and stalls on the Plaza de la Corredera you'll find tyre-soled sandals, iron rings for hanging up flower-pots, barbecue utensils and wickerwork chairs, baskets, hampers and linen chests. Near the Ayuntamiento the *guarnicionería* Rafael Estevez Lopez (Calle San Pablo 6) sells saddles, riding tackle and woollen blankets while the Zoco, the old souk opposite the Synagogue on Calle Judíos 5, is the headquarters for Córdoba Association of Craftsmen, many of whom have their shops here. It is a good place to browse for silver filigree, jewellery, leather work and ceramics.

Granada

Granada's souvenirs play heavily on the city's Moorish past – embossed leather, marquetry chessboards, inlaid furniture, and a distinctive blue and green pottery known as *fajalauza* are the most obvious examples.

The Albaicín is the best place to chance upon these but you'll also find them in the Cuesta de Gomérez at the foot of Alhambra hill. Woven products from the Alpujarras mountains are worth looking at – the Tejidos Fortuny workshop (Plaza de Fortuny 1) has attractive rugs and wall-hangings.

Granada's main shopping area lies south and east of the cathedral. Calle Pescadería has small friendly shops selling meats and cheeses and a stall opposite the Bar Boca has good *fajalauza* pottery. You may find interesting bargains in the Alcaicería (the old silk-market). For a spot of self-indulgence, buy a box of mouth-watering cakes from Flor y Nata (Calle Mesones 51) or Lopez Mezquita (Calle Reyes Católicos 29).

Markets

Markets are the best place to buy fresh food from the countryside: honey, goats' cheese, spiced meats, snails, seafood, olives, nuts, bread and fruit. Produce markets usually start early and pack up around 1pm.

In **Seville** every district hosts its own daily fresh produce market – there is one in the Plaza de la Encarnación and another across the Triana bridge (turn right), on the site of the old Inquisition headquarters. There is a small weekday arts-and-crafts market outside El Corte Inglés in the Plaza del Duque de la Victoria. In the north of the city there's a centuries-old flea market on Thursday in Calle Feria known as 'El Jueves'. Nearby, in the Alameda de Hércules a similar bric-a-brac market takes place on Sunday mornings. At the same time there's a bird and pet market (including silkworms) in the Plaza de la Alfalfa, and a stamp-and-coin collector's market in the Plaza del Cabildo.

In **Córdoba** the main market venue is the Corredera. In the week a covered *mercado* sells fresh produce while stalls outside sell fabric, clothes, plants and household items. On weekends this becomes a flea market.

Granada's nicest market is in the Plaza Larga in the Albaicín, but you'll find a better range in the Mercado de San Agustín on the southwest corner of the cathedral.

Left: ceramics are a popular buy

EATING OUT

n Seville, Córdoba and Granada, eating out
s big business. Mornings are when work
ets done, and breakfast is but a meditative
noment. Anything goes as long as it's quick:
offee and brandy, chocolate and *churros*
extrusions of sweet battered dough), bread
lunked in olive oil – all taken standing at
ne bar. By 11am the mood shifts cakewards
r to an elevenses ice-cream, but by noon
ne emphasis changes again as the bar staff
tart putting out their freshly made *tapas*.

By 7pm it's time for the *paseo* and an obli-
atory ice cream, after which the *tapas*
ppear again around 8pm. Restaurants are in
ction by 9pm but rarely full before 10pm
· at weekends they will still be serving new
ustomers at midnight. After dinner, it is
me for an *oloroso* (sherry) and a sticky cake.

What to Eat

eville claims to have invented *tapas* (snacks
nd appetisers) and can even tell you the
ar where this national custom originated:
l Rinconcillo (near the Santa Catalina
hurch, Calle Gerona 40), where the staff
leveloped the habit of covering a glass of
ino with a *tapa* (lid) of ham. Today *tapas*
re found everywhere and can be anything
rom a saucer of spiced olives or some
lices of *jamón serrano* (mountain ham)
o a gourmet dish of oranges, onions and

bacalao (dried cod), or a hot terracotta dish
full of *paella*.

A *tapa* or *porción* is simply a taster, while
a *ración* is a small dish, often cooked. Lunch
is the best time for *raciones* – the daily menu
will be written on a board or the dishes just
put out on the counter. Often the bill turns out
to be as costly as a meal, but the taste of *fino*
and *gambas* (prawns), or a *cerveza* (beer) and
boquerones (anchovies in garlic and vine-
gar), is quintessential Spain. If you're a serious *tapas*-addict, head straight for Seville
to investigate Modesto (Calle Cano y Cueto
13; tel: 954 426 456) or the Hostería del Lau-
rel (Plaza de los Venerables; www.hosteria
dellaurel.com; tel: 954 220 295) in the Barrio Santa Cruz and Casa Manolo (Calle San
Jorge, 16; tel: 954 338 208) in Triana.

Most bars have an array of mountain
hams and spiced sausages suspended from
the ceiling, all tagged like prize antiques.
You could also sample some *salchichón*
(salami), *chorizo* (red spicy sausage) or *mor-
cilla* (blood sausage), while *habas con jamón*
(broad beans with ham) is a typical Granada
dish. *Gazpacho* is another famous Andalusian creation, a chilled soup based on bread
and olive oil and flavoured with vegetables
and herbs – usually tomatoes, garlic and
peppers. The Córdobans make their own,
thicker version called *salmorejo*, while *ajo
blanco* is a white soup, based on garlic,
almonds and fruit, from Málaga.

Above: courtyard dining

Heavenly Sweets

Sweets, pastries, cakes and biscuits have been made in Andalusia's convents since the Reconquest, a sweet-toothed tradition inherited from the Arabs. Today they can still be bought from the nuns.

The recipe for *yemas* is centuries old, originally made from the surplus egg yolks donated to the convents after the whites had been used to clarify the wines of Jerez and Montilla (the albumen binds unwanted particles in the wine, allowing their easy removal).

Biscuits flavoured with honey, cinnamon, sesame, ginger or almonds are less sugary – try some *alfajores* or *polvorones* made by the Convento de Santa Isabel de los Angeles in Córdoba (near the Palacio de Viana). For a selection of sweets from Seville's many convent-confectioneries visit El Torno *(see page 29)*, situated in the Plaza del Cabildo.

In restaurants look for regional dishes signposted with words such as *andaluz, a la granadina* or *alpujarreño* (from the Alpujarras mountains). Some chefs embrace Andalusia's Moorish heritage with dishes combining the sweet and the savoury, perhaps by using honey, fruit or raisins to spice meat and poultry. Dishes cooked in sherry or incorporating almonds are common, as are country stews (*cocido* or the simpler *puchero*), which might combine chicken, ham, sausage and egg with *garbanzos* (chick-peas), rice or potatoes.

Despite fields full of vegetables, few seem to make it onto Spanish menus. Asparagus, artichokes, aubergines or eggplant *(berenjenas)* and peppers do pop up but salad is a more common complement to a main dish. There is nearly always a *revuelto* (scrambled egg dish) on the menu, perhaps mixed with salmon, mushrooms, spinach or asparagus. *Tortilla sacromonte* is a Granada dish in which an omelette is combined with ham, peas and assorted offal.

Having access to both the Atlantic and Mediterranean coasts Andalusia has plentiful fresh fish and seafood. Tuna has been a staple ingredient since pre-Roman times and sardines, swordfish *(pez espada)* and

skate *(raya)* feature on menus. Cuts from large fish are often served with a saffron paprika or tomato sauce, while *zarzuela* is a fish stew with a spicy tomato sauce. Fried fish can be bought in take-away *freidurías*.

Desserts always include a choice of fresh fruit or ice cream, but in better-quality restaurants you'll be able to dither over *tarta de almendras* (almond tart), *crema de membrillo con queso* (quince jelly with cheese), *pastel cordobés* (puff pastry with candied fruit) or the *tocino de cielo* (caramel custard) from Cádiz.

Drinks

Andalusia's most famous drink is sherry, a fortified wine from Jerez de la Frontera. The Spanish will drink it with a meal and whenever the occasion arises. It is also the classic complement to *tapas*.

Fino is the most common drink – a light, dry sherry, always served chilled. *Amontillado* is mellower with a nutty flavour and an amber hue. *Oloroso* is mature, dark and rich, often drunk as a dessert wine. *Palo cortado* is richer than *amontillado* but lighter than *oloroso*. You should also try *manzanilla*, a *fino* made in Sanlúcar de Barrameda on the Atlantic coast, where the salty sea air gives it a distinctive tang.

Andalusian wines are few and come a poor second to their sherries. Exceptions are the excellent strong white Montilla-Moriles, produced in Córdoba (*amontillado* means 'like a Montilla'), and the sweet dessert wines made in Málaga from muscatel grapes.

Brandies are also produced around Jerez, varying from the cheap, highly addictive Soberano to the luxurious Carlos I. There are also assorted firewaters variously flavoured with almonds, cherries, oranges, apricots and anis. Spanish measures of spirits are liberal, so beware.

The predominant beer is made by Cruzcampo – *una caña* is normally taken to mean a small glass of draught, *una cerveza* a large glass or a bottle. *Horchata* is an almond milk while *zumos* are fruit juices freshly-squeezed before your eyes – try a mix of *naranja* (orange) and *limon* (lemon). Bottled water is either *agua con gas* (with bubbles) or *sin gas* (without). If you want to avoid ice ask for your drink *sin hielo*. Black coffee is *café solo*, white *con leche* and *cortado* somewhere in between. Cheers is *salud!*

Where to Eat

Restaurant recommendations are also included in the individual itineraries earlier in this book. Remember that it is quite acceptable to order just a starter or single course. Don't ask for the *menú del día* (menu of the day) when you really mean the *especialidad del día* (speciality of the day): the first is a basic, low price set-meal; the latter is whatever's fresh and in season. Lastly, keep some cash in reserve as not all restaurants take credit cards.

Price Guide

For a three-course meal with house wine for one person:
€€€: more than €40
€€: €20–40
€: under €20

Seville

Casa Robles
Calle Alvarez Quintero, 58
Tel: 954 213150
A Seville classic, serving regional specialities in a cosy dining room. The bar is famous for its *tapas*. All major cards. **€€**

Casablanca
Calle Zaragoza, 50
Tel: 954 224 698
You have to fight your way through the tiny packed bar to get to the small dining room in the back to sample its justly famous seafood dishes. There is no menu, so just point at what you want. Closed Sun. Some credit cards. **€€€**

Corral del Agua
Callejón de Agua, 6
Tel: 954 224 841
In the Barrio Santa Cruz, this elegant restaurant occupies a restored 18th-century house, centred on a pleasant patio with plenty of potted plants and a fountain. Most major cards. Closed Sunday. **€€€**

Egaña Oriza
Calle San Fernando, 41
Tel: 954 227 211
The modern Basque-Andalusian cuisine in this attractive restaurant next to the Murillo gardens, behind the Alcázar, has earned this venue a reputation as one of the finest eating spots in southern Spain. Closed Sun and Sat lunchtime. All major cards. **€€€**

Enrique Becerra
Calle Gamazo, 2
Tel: 954 213 049
This small restaurant in an old Seville town house serves traditional Andalusian dishes, and has a very popular *tapas* bar. Closed Sun. All major cards. **€€**

El Buzo
Calle Antonio Diaz, 5
Tel: 954 210 231
Famous for its much-photographed blue tile façade. The speciality here is fresh fish. Some cards accepted. **€€**

El Cairo
Calle Reyes Católicos 13
Tel: 954 213 089
The dinning room is located above the popular tapas bar. Meat dishes, including excellent steak, are on offer, but the spe-

Right: *tapas* time

ciality of the house is the excellent grilled sea bream or sea bass. Some cards aare accepted. €€

Hostería del Laurel
Plaza de los Venerables 5
Tel: 954 220 295
On a small square in the Barrio de Santa Cruz, this picturesque establishment is enormously popular for its tapas and good-value dining. All major cards. €€

La Albahaca
Plaza de Santa Cruz 12
Tel: 954 220 714
One of Seville's prettiest restaurants, in the heart of the Santa Cruz area. The decor and the food mix Andalusian, French and Basque influences. Reservations essential. Closed Sun. All major cards. €€€

La Taberna del Alabardero
Calle Zaragoza, 20
Tel: 954 502 721
One of a well-known chain of Spanish restaurants (run by a priest), serving Basque cuisine in a typical Seville setting centred on a courtyard. All major cards. €€€

Las Piletas
Marques de Paradas, 28
Tel: 95 422 0404
Traditional bullfighting bar-restaurant popular among localst. The meat and fish are always good, but ask the waiters about the

daily recommendations. You may like to combine a meal here with a visit to Casa Carmen, a low-key flamenco venue next door. €€

Meson Don Raimundo
Calle Argote de Molina 26
Tel: 954 223 355
Near the cathedral, this colourfully decorated restaurant offers a classic Seville experience. Specialises in meat and game, served in generous portions. All major cards. €€

Ox's
Calle Betis, 61
Tel: 954 279585
Reputed to serve the best steak in Seville and they have good charcoal-grilled fish too, in a small dining room decorated with understated elegance. Closed Mon and evenings Sun. All major cards. €€€

Taberna La Taurina
Calle Trajano, 44
Tel: 954 330 901
This large, popular bar decorated with bullfight posters serves a good range of tapas and snacks, and they also feature an inexpensive three-course menu at midday. Closed Sunday. No credit cards. €

Cordoba
Almudaina
Campo Santo de los Mártires, 1
Tel: 957 474 342
Installed in a 15th-century house near the Alcázar, this restaurant serves modern variations of local recipes, using fresh produce. The various dining rooms are tastefully decorated, centred on an inner courtyard. Closed Sunday in summer. All major cards. €€€

Bodegas Campos
Los Lineros 32
Tel: 957 497 643
Colourful restaurant in a former wine cellar near the Plaza del Potro, decorated like an upmarket tavern, serving variations on classical Cordoba and Spanish dishes. No dinner Sun. Most major cards. €€€

Left: restaurant in the Barrio de Santa Cruz, Seville

Casa Pepe de la Judería
Calle Romero 1
Tel: 957 200 744/957 200 766
At the entrance to the Judería, this typical Andalusian town house, decorated with paintings, has a pleasant interior courtyard. Traditional Andalusian fare. All major cards. €€

Círculo Taurino
Calle Manuel María de Arjona, 1
Tel: 957 481 862
Bullfighting is the theme, and *rabo de toro* (braised bulls tail) stars on the menu along with other Andalusian classics. Mainly Spanish clientele. Most major cards. €€

El Blasón
Calle José Zorrilla, 11
Tel: 957 480 625
An old inn situated in Córdoba's modern town, and under the same management as the famous El Caballo Rojo *(see below)*. Specialises in a slightly more modern cuisine. All major cards. €€

El Burladero
Calleja de la Hoguera, 5
Tel: 957 472 719
Picturesquely located in the heart of the Judería and with a cobbled courtyard for outdoor dining. Serves reasonable Andalusian food, including game. Most major cards. €€

El Caballo Rojo
Cardenal Herrero, 28
Tel: 957 478 001
Near the Mosque, this esteemed and long-established restaurant is known for unusual Moorish and Sephardic preparations, based on medieval recipes, such as *Cordero a la miel* (lamb in honey). All major cards. €€€

El Churrasco
Calle Romero, 16
Tel: 957 290 819
One of Córdoba's top dining spots, in an old house with courtyard in the Judería), excellent service and menu, incorporating Andalusian classics. All major cards. €€

Federación de Peñas
Calle Conde y Luque, 8
Tel: 957 475 427
At the northern fringes of the Judería, this friendly restaurant is a good budget option for traditional fare. Some cards. €

Granada
Chikito
Plaza del Campillo, 9
Tel: 958 223 364
A long-established restaurant (the poet Lorca was a regular), serving good Spanish dishes such as *rabo de toro* (braised oxtail stew) along with more innovative fare. Best to reserve. Most major cards. €€€

Cunini
Calle Pescadería, 14
Tel: 958 250 777
This friendly restaurant near the cathedral is the best place for fresh seafood in Granada. Closed Monday. All major cards. €€

La Mimbre
Avenida del Generalife, S.n
Tel: 958 222 276
Small restaurant in an unbeatable location at the foot of the Alhambra walls, with outdoor dining in summer. Granadan specialities. €€

Rincón de Lorca
Calle Tablas, 4
Tel: 958 253 211
Located in the Hotel Reina Cristina, this is one of Granada's most reliable restaurants, serving regional dishes prepared with a modern touch. All major cards. €€

Sevilla
Calle Oficios, 12
Tel: 958 221 223
This Granada classic opened in 1930. Close to the cathedral, it is a good place to sample traditional dishes such as *Habas con jamón* (cured ham with broad beans) or *Tortilla Sacromonte* (omelette with lambs brains, ham and vegetables). Closed on Mon and Sun evenings. All major cards. €€

NIGHTLIFE

Flamenco

Flamenco's origins are mysterious. Elements of ancient Indian, Arab and Jewish music have been detected in its sorrowful and discordant songs and dances. It was the creation of Andalusia's gypsy communities, particularly those that settled between Seville and Cádiz. As these *gitanos* sought work throughout Spain new local styles developed: by the late 19th century flamenco had shed its peasant image and had its own established rules and repertoire.

Today flamenco is crossing over into jazz and rock, and still evolving. Because it is by nature impulsive and improvised, it does not lend itself to repeated public performance. But every city has its flamenco tourist shows, variously described as *tablaos* or *zambras*. They perform the fast, light-hearted cante chico rather than the slow, knife-in-the-heart *cante jondo*. Most hotels sell tickets, inclusive of transport and a drink.

For something more authentic, try one of the smaller bars or clubs (called *peñas*) where flamenco enthusiasts hang out. Seville is especially well-provided in this respect. Performances are usually impromptu, initiated among a group of clients, usually late at nigh after a certain amount of alcohol . One club that stages top quality flamenco in Seville is La Carbonería *(see page 76)*.

Flamenco Clubs
Seville
El Arenal
Calle Rodo, 7
Tel: 954 421 6492
Located in an 18th-century house. Has two shows daily; dinner (optional) is served during the first show.

El Palacio Andaluz
Avenida María Auxiliadora, 18
Tel: 954 534 720
Located in a large theatre. There are tables at the back if you want to enjoy dinner during the show. Opens daily, with two shows.

Casa Carmen
Calle Marqués de Paradas
Tel: 954 2142 889
Delightfully low-key establishment near the river. A good place to sample flamenco.

Los Gallos
Plaza de Santa Cruz, 11
Tel: 954 216 981
By far the best of Seville's tourist *tabla*. Two shows a night.

Córdoba
Mesón la Bulería
Calle Pedro López, 3
Tel: 957 483 839
Stages flamenco singing and dance. Closed in winter.

Tablao El Cardenal
Calle Torrijos, 10
Tel: 957 483 112
Córdoba's best flamenco *tablao* in a 16th-century building next to the mosque.

Granada
El Corral del Carbón
Calle Mariana Pineda
In summer flamenco is occasionally staged here, in the courtyard of one of the city's oldest Moorish buildings. Contact the tourist office (at the same location) for details.

El Corral del Príncipe
Campo del Príncipe
Tel: 958 228 088
Popular with the Spanish, as well as tourists.

Jardines Neptuno
Calle Arabial
Tel: 958 522 533
Granada's most popular venue. Decent performances, but aimed primarily at tourists.

María la Canastera
Camino del Sacromonte, 89
Tel: 958 121 183
One of the better gypsy *zambras* (cave performances) in the Sacromonte Hills.

Reina Mora
Mirador de San Cristobal
Tel: 958 401 265
This long-established club is located at the top of the Albaicin.

Performing Arts

Andalusia has a good range of concerts and theatre performances, and many new venues have opened in recent years. Seville has a year-round programme, although the pace slackens in summer, while Córdoba's Gran Teatro has regular concerts and is the venue for the International Guitar Festival at the beginning of July. The biggest cultural bash, however, is the International Music and Dance Festival in Granada (last week of June and first week of July).

Theatres and Concert Halls
Seville
Auditorio de La Cartuja
Isla de la Cartuja
Tel: 954 216 233
Seating 11,000 spectators, this open-air auditorium has occasional rock concerts and dance performances.

Hospital de los Venerables
Plaza de los Venerables
Tel: 954 562 696
Organ recitals are staged in the chapel of this 17th-century hospice in the Barrio Santa Cruz.

Sala La Imperdible
Plaza San Antonio de Padua, 9
Tel: 954 388 219
Seville's best venue for alternative theatre.

Teatro Alameda
Calle Crédito, 13
Tel: 954 900 164
Stages frequent plays for children.

Teatro Central
Isla de la Cartuja
Tel: 954 460 780
Modern venue featuring theatre, dance and top jazz and contemporary music.

Teatro de la Maestranza
Paseo Colón
Tel: 954 223 344
Seville's grand, modern opera house stages opera, symphony orchestra concerts, dance, classical and contemporary music.

Teatro Imperial
Calle Sierpes, 25
Tel: 954 226 878
The place to go if you want to see a performance of Zarzuela (Spanish light opera).

Teatro Lope de Vega
Avenida María Luisa
Tel: 954 590 853
Occasional recitals of traditional Spanish singing, but mostly stages plays in Spanish.

Córdoba
Gran Teatro
Avenida Gran Capitán, 3
Tel: 957 480 237
Top venue for music, flamenco and dance

Granada
Auditorio Manuel de Falla
Paseo de los Mártires
Tel: 958 222 188
Home to the Granada Symphony Orchestra.

Teatro de La Alhambra
Calle Molinos, 56
Tel: 958 220 447
Regular plays, concerts and dance.

Above Right: a passionate dance

Bars and Nightclubs

With its large university population, Seville has countless venues that stay open till the small hours. The best place to check what's on is the monthly *El Giraldillo* magazine, available free from tourist offices or for sale at newsstands. The bars in the Barrio Santa Cruz tend to lean towards flamenco. A more contemporary scene exists in Triana, especially on Calle Betis, alongside the river. Another key nightlife zone is the Alameda de Hércules, which has plenty of bars and clubs for gays, straights or both.

Córdoba's nightlife is tamer. In winter the liveliest scene is around the Plaza Tablero or along the Calle Cruz Conde. In summer, action shifts to open air venues along the Avenida El Brillante, on the northern fringes of the city, and in El Arenal, near the river.

In Granada the streets in the vicinity of the University (Calle Pedro Antonio de Alarcón) set the party pace. Bars around the Albaicín, the Plaza Nueva, the Paseo Padre Manjón and the Campo del Príncipe are also populars.

Clubs and Discos

Seville

Antique
Matemático Rey Pastor y Castro
Isla de la Cartuja
Tel: 954 462 207
Disco in a former Expo 92 pavilion, with a large dance floor. Appeals to a young crowd.

Catedral
Cuesta del Rosario, 12
Tel: 954 219 029
Central disco, with regular theme nights.

El Coto
Calle Luis Montoto, 118
Tel: 954 571 072
Exclusive discod.

Fun Club
Alameda de Hércules, 86
Live rock performances are staged here on most weekends.

La Carbonería
Calle Levies, 20
Tel: 954 214 460
In a former coal yard in the Barrio Santa Cruz, this is a top venue for flamenco, soul, blues, jazz and ethnic music.

Naima
Calle Trajano, 47
Tel: 954 382 485
Animated jazz club, not far from Alameda de Hércules. Regular jam sessions.

Sevilla Salsa
Calle Castilla, 137
Tel: 954 342 204
Latin rhythms in the Triana area.

Weekend
Calle Torneo, 43
Tel: 954 375 012
Live flamenco, jazz and Latin music.

Córdoba

Club Málaga
Calle Malaga
Popular with jazz and blues fans.

Zahira
Calle Conde Robledo
Córdoba's most popular disco.

Granada

Barrio Latino
San Juan de Dios, 12
Salsa, merengue and other Latin rhythms.

Eshavira
Calle Postigo de Cuna, 2
Music bar, focusing on jazz and flamenco.

Granada 10
Calle Cárcel Baja 10
Tel: 958 224 001
Granada's top discotheque.

Sala Cha
Ancha de Gracia, 4
Late-night dance club.

SPORTS & ACTIVITIES

Outdoor Activities

Andalusia's sierras lend themselves to a number of outdoor sports and activities.

Hiking, Biking and Riding

These sport are especially wellcatered for in the Sierra Subbética in Córdoba, and, in Granada, the Sierra Nevada and the Alpujarras. You can rent bikes in Córdoba (and sign up for a guided bike tour of the area) at Córdoba La Llana en Bici on Calle Lucano 20, next to the mosque. El Mirador riding centre, near the Parador, offers horses for hire, plus organised riding tours of the mountains north of Córdoba.

In Granada, a wide range of organised outdoors activities are offered by Ocio Aventura Granada (tel. 958 571 874; www.ocioaventura.com). For hiking, rock climbing and mountain biking in the Alpujarras contact Nevadensis (Pampaneira; tel. 958 763 127; www.nevadensis.com) and Rustic Blue (Bubión; tel 958 763 381; www.rusticblue.com). For organised horse treks in the mountains, try Cabalgar Rutas Alternativas (Bubión; tel. 958 763 135).

In Seville, bikes can be hired from Sevilla Mágica, on Calle Miguel Mañara.

Skiing

In winter, the main activity in Sierra Nevada is **skiing**. There's also snowboarding and dog sleigh rides. For information on winter sports contact the Sierra Nevada ski resort on 958 249 111; www.sierranevadaski.com.

Paragliding

In summer, Sierra Nevada is one of Spain's best venues for **paragliding**. The most active club is Draco (Carretera de Granada Km. 8, Pinos Genil; tel. 958 488 560).

Watersports

Seville is a prime venue for **rowing and kayaking**, having hosted the World Championships in 2002. The centre of rowing activity is the Centro de Alto Rendimiento, on Isla de la Cartuja (tel. 954 461 400). The Centro Municipal de Vela sailing club (Puerta Triana, s/n; tel. 954 460 202) organises courses in sailing and windsurfing.

Golf

There are four **golf** courses in the Seville area, the oldest being the Real Club Pineda, founded in 1939 (tel. 954 613 399). The best courses are the Real Club de Golf de Sevilla (tel. 954 124 301) and the Club Zaudin, designed by Gary Player (tel. 954 154 160). Serious golfers will find more courses to chose from on the Costa del Sol.

Spectator Sports

Seville has two **football** teams, locked in bitter rivalry: Sevilla, who play at the Estadio Sánchez Pijuán in the east of the city, and Real Betis, at the Estadio Benito Villamarín in the south. Matches are normally played on Saturday or Sunday – any local paper will tell you when the next fixture is.

Seville also has a top **basketball** team, Caja San Fernando, which play at the Palacio de Deportes de San Pablo on Avenida Kansas City.

Right: fun in the surf

CALENDAR OF EVENTS

The Andalusians joke that every day, somewhere in the region, there's a fiesta going on. When you add in the boisterous stream of cultural events that major cities such as Seville, Córdoba and Granada stage through the year it is inevitable that your visit will coincide with a religious holiday, local fair or arts festival.

To find out what's on look out for posters or ask in a hotel or Tourist Office. The following calendar is intended as a rough guide. Always check dates before setting out – in Spain everything is a moveable fiesta.

January

The old year is normally seen off with a cacophony of fireworks and car horns. Tradition says you should swallow a grape (and a sip of *cava* if you're quick) for each strike of the midnight clock. Needless to say **Año Nuevo** (New Year's Day) is a public holiday.
2 January Granada celebrates the victory of the Catholic Monarchs over the city's Moorish rulers in 1492 with the Día de la Toma (Day of the Capture).
5 January The Cabalgata del los Reyes Magos (Calvacade of the Three Kings) is celebrated with with processions. Next day (6 January) is a public holiday marking Epiphany (Twelfth Night), the day when Spanish children get their Christmas presents.

February

1 February Granada holds a fiesta in honour of its patron saint San Cecilio, including a pilgrimage to the Sacromonte catacombs.
28 February Andalusia Day, a public holiday.

Since the death of Franco, February in Spain has also meant **Carnaval**, an excuse for floats, fireworks, dancing and irreverence.

In February or March Seville stages its annual Festival of Ancient Music.

March / April

First week of March Granada stages an International Tango Festival.
Semana Santa (Holy Week). A serious religious celebration, with everything closed on Holy Thursday and Good Friday. Events in Seville are renowned for their dramatic spectacle, but Holy Week is observed with similar panache in Málaga and with equal solemnity in Córdoba and Granada.

Events commence on Palm Sunday when religious and social organisations known as *cofradías* (brotherhoods) carry statues and images from their chapels towards the cathedral. Ornately-decorated floats known as *pasos* transport these figureheads, and behind the *pasos* march *nazarenos*, penitents wearing conical hoods and carrying candles.

In Seville over 100 such processions take place in the course of the week. To witness the most impressive of these tableaux – such as those of El Gran Poder, La Esperanza de Triana and La Macarena which pass through the city in the early hours of Good Friday – consult timetables and official routes published in daily newspapers like *ABC*.
19 March This is San José (St Joseph's Day), a public holiday in some towns.
Mid-April Seville ignites again with its Feria (April Fair), a week-long fiesta of drinking, dancing and bullfighting with horse parades and Andalusian pageantry. Most participants dress for the occasion – *señoritas* in bright flamenco costume cling to horsemen in wide-brimmed hats, Sevillian ladies bedecked with flowers and mantillas parade in carriages.

Above: all the fun of the *feria*

April onwards Seville stages a programme of theatre, dance, exhibitions and music known as 'Cita en Sevilla' (April–June).

May / June

Early May The Día del Trabajo (Labour Day) is a public holiday. Early May is also when the *Cruces de Mayo* (Crosses of May) appear in many towns, elaborately decorated with flowers to herald the arrival of spring. They are best seen in Granada (especially in the Albaicín) or in Córdoba, and form the focus for a fiesta on 3 May.

This first week is also when the sherry capital Jerez de la Frontera holds its annual Horse Fair and Granada holds an International Drama Festival.

Mid May Córdoba comes alive with its charming Festival de los Patios (Patio Festival) usually held in the first fortnight. This is when the Córdobans open up their flower-filled courtyards to all-comers. Concerts and flamenco performances are also held.

End of May Córdoba's festivities culminates in its May Feria, when the streets are graced by elegant horse-riders in Andalusian costume. Every third year the city also stages a national flamenco competition.

30 May Seville honours San Fernando.

Pentecost (Whitsun) at least half a million pilgrims descend on El Rocío, a village north of Las Marismas, the marshland at the mouth of the Guadalquivir river. It is the biggest *romería* (country festival) in Spain.

Corpus Christi (late May or early June) is a public holiday. In Seville and Córdoba choirboys in medieval dress perform set dances before the Cathedral altar, while in Granada the occasion inspires the city's principal fiesta with processions and bullfights, as well as flamenco competitions and a fair.

June / July

Mid-June–mid-July Granada stages its International Festival of Music and Dance which attracts top stars from the world of classical music, jazz and ballet.

Córdoba holds a prestigious International Guitar Festival in the first half of July with classical, flamenco and Latin music. In Seville there is an International Festival of Theatre and Dance.

August

15 August Asunción (Assumption) is marked by a public holiday, and in Seville by the Feast of the Virgen de los Reyes.

Last week The Río Guadalquivir is honoured with a festival in the sherry town of Sanlúcar de Barrameda – events include flamenco competitions and horse-racing along the beach.

September

8 September Córdoba celebrates its patron saint, the Virgen de la Fuensanta.

Last Sunday Fiesta in Granada held in honour of the city's patroness, Nuestra Señora las Angustias

29 September in Granada's Albaicín San Miguel is honoured with a procession up to the hermitage San Miguel el Alto.

In even-numbered years Seville stages a Festival of Flamenco at the end of the month.

October

12 October Christopher Columbus's 'discovery' of America is celebrated with a public holiday, Día de la Hispanidad.

24 October Córdoba holds a festival to honour San Rafael.

November

1 November Todos los Santos (All Saints' Day) is a public holiday.

Seville and Granada stage International Jazz Festivals in November.

December

6 December Constitution Day is a public holiday.

8 December Inmaculada Concepción (the Immaculate Conception).

Christmas Navidad is a time for parties, which go on in earnest for the full 12 days.

28 December Spaniards celebrate their equivalent of April Fool's Day, Día de los Inocentes (Day of the Holy Innocents).

Practical Information

TRAVEL ESSENTIALS

When to Go

Spring is the best time to visit Andalusia: any week from early March, when the orange trees come into blossom, to late May, when the fields and road sides are ablaze with wild flowers. This is also the main fiesta season, when the streets of towns and villages are decorated with flowers and strings of coloured lights.

Accommodation during Seville's Feria and also during Semana Santa (Easter) sells out a year in advance despite the fact that prices are around treble what they are for the rest of the year. For a quieter break try and slip into a week either side of these spring festivities, or come in autumn – mid–September to October when temperatures are very pleasant *(see below)*.

Climate

During summer the Guadalquivir valley is extremely hot, with temperatures in Seville and Córdoba soaring to over 38°C (100°F) in June and July. Ecija, almost mid-way between Seville and Córdoba, is known as *la sartén* (the frying-pan) of Spain. Autumn is a slow cooling-off period as the baked land recovers, and winters in Seville and Córdoba are mild (12°C/53°F). In Granada transitions are more abrupt – spring and autumn are short, summers hot and dry (25°C, 77°F) and winters cold (6°C, 43°F). Rain tends to fall between October and March, often in sudden heavy downpours, but for most of the year the sun shines.

Time Difference

Along with the rest of Europe, Spain is one hour ahead of Britain. Spanish Summer Time runs from the last Sunday in March to the last Sunday in October.

Documents

All visitors require a valid passport or, if a citizen of an EU country, a national identity card). Visitors from outside the EU, US, Australia and New Zealand must obtain a visa before entering Spain. Motorists will need an international driving permit or an EU format three-part driving licence, along with adequate insurance.

Money Matters

The Euro (€) replaced the peseta as Spanish currency in 2002. One Euro equals 100 cents.

Health

No vaccinations are required. The European Health Insurance Card (EHIC), which replaced the old E111 form, entitles EU citizens to free emergency medical treatment upon presentation (see www.dh.gov.uk/travellers). If you need to use the EHIC be sure that the doctor or hospital works within the state sector and be sure to state that you want to be treated under the EHIC scheme. You should also be aware that the EHIC will not cover all eventualities, so you are advised to take out private medical insurance.

Clothing

Seville, Córdoba and Granada are all smart, fashionable cities and their citizens enjoy dressing well. In the summer you'll need something warm for air-conditioned buildings; in winter a jumper and water-proof coat will be necessary.

Left: for post-cards and letters
Right: a nippy way to get around

Electricity
220 Volts. Sockets take round two-point plugs (European size). UK appliances will need an adaptor.

Photography
If using a conventional rather than a digital camera, you should note that film is expensive in Spain and some types are not widely available. It is best to bring it with you.

Customs
There are no restrictions on the import of currencies. You can bring in personal belongings and souvenirs, as well as food for your own consumption. There are no restrictions on quantities of duty-paid goods that can be imported/exported from other EU countries, as long as they are for personal use only.

Visitors arriving from outside the EU can import (duty-free) 200 cigarettes, 50 cigars or 250g tobacco; 2 litres of wine, or 1 litre of spirits; 500g of coffee beans; 50g of perfume and 0.25 litres of toilet water. Tobacco and alcohol allowances only apply to travellers aged 17 and over.

On Departure
In recent years Spain has had its share of air-traffic delays, so always confirm your return flight.

GETTING THERE

By Air
Iberia (tel: 020-7830 0011 in the UK; www. iberia.com) operates scheduled flights from London to Seville, Jerez de la Frontera, Málaga and Granada – some flights involve a stop in Madrid or Barcelona. British Airways (www.ba.com) flies into Málaga, Seville, Jerez de la Frontera and Gibraltar.

The cheapest fares from the UK will probably be with one of the budget airlines. Ryanair (www.ryanair.com) flies into Jerez, Seville and Granada (useful if you want to fly into Seville but return from Granada), as well as Málaga, while EasyJet (www. easyjet.com) flies into Málaga from various airports across the UK.

Travellers from the USA will need to fly to Madrid and take a connecting flight from there.

Seville airport (San Pablo) is 12km (7½ miles) east of the centre. There is a regular bus connection (30–40-minute trip) into the city or you can take a taxi for around €20. For Airport Information tel: 95 444 90 00; Iberia Information, tel: 902 400 500.

Granada airport is 16 km (10 miles) west of the city (tel: 958 24 52 00). Taxis cost around €20 to the city centre.

Package Deals
Numerous travel companies offer tailor-made holidays combining Seville, Córdoba and Granada. Seville is also featured by several city-break specialists.

By Rail
National rail networks offer through-fare deals to Andalusia from the UK (contact Rail Europe, tel: 08705 848848; www.raileurope. co.uk), but you will need to change in Madrid. The high-speed AVE rail link has reduced the journey-time between Madrid and Seville to just 2¾ hours, with trains throughout the day and just one stop, in Córdoba. If you are travelling extensively in Spain it may be worth buying an InterRail card (www.interrail.net), or the Tarjeta Turistica, issued by the national rail network, RENFE.

Rail travellers can also tour Andalusia in elegant 1920s style by taking the luxurious Al-Andalus Express, which is known for its gourmet food (bookable in the UK through Mundi Color, tel: 020-7828 6021).

By Road from the UK
British coach operators offer services to Seville: details from Eurolines UK (tel: 08705 808080; www.eurolines.co.uk).

If you plan to take your own vehicle, consider cutting down on the driving by sailing from Plymouth to Santander with Brittany Ferries (tel: 08705 360360) or Portsmouth to Bilbao (tel: 08705 202020) with P&O Ferries.

GETTING AROUND

Seville is ideal for a short break and the best place in Andalusia for street-life, shopping and *tapas* bar-hopping. Córdoba is easily reached from Seville by rail or road and the two cities form a natural pair. Granada and the snow-capped Sierra Nevada are a refreshing contrast to the hot plains of the Guadalquivir valley.

Maps and Guides

The map accompanying this guide contains town plans of all three cities plus a regional map. If you are touring by car and require a larger area than the regional map shows, Michelin map No 446 *Andalusia and the Costa del Sol* is a good choice.

By Car

Drive on the right. Seat belts are compulsory and motoring offences earn on-the-spot fines. In rural areas petrol stations may close on Sundays or for a siesta; most, but not all, take credit cards.

If you take back roads in the countryside you'll have a more rewarding trip. In the cities you'll just have to take a road that isn't blocked or dug up. The Spanish treat inner-city driving as if it was a motorised bullfight, which means they see it as an art-form and therefore something to be enjoyed.

Car Hire

Compared with most other European countries, car hire in Spain is inexpensive. Many tour companies offer good-value fly-drive deals, and, if you know your requirements, it's simplest to book before you arrive.

It's also easy to hire cars in Spain, although some firms will not rent to drivers under 21 or with less than a year's experience. In any case, hire companies will need to see your passport and international driving licence or national driving licence. It is sensible to pay a little extra for Collision Damage Waiver and Personal Accident insurance in addition to the statutory Third Party insurance. Parking is problematic in the cities, and hotels will often charge extra for it, so check on availability and charges when booking.

Motorbikes and mopeds offer another way of getting around and are easily rented – the age limits are 18 and 16 respectively.

By Train

The rail network is operated by RENFE *(see below for contact details)*. There are frequent trains between Seville and Córdoba (just a 30-minute journey on the high-speed AVE but longer on other trains). Connections from either of these cities to Granada or Málaga (3–5 hours) go via the notorious Bobadilla Junction and normally involve a change of train, so it can be quicker by coach *(see page 84)*. The train journey from Málaga to Bobadilla is spectacular.

The speediest type of train in Spain is the high-speed AVE, followed by the Talgos and TER, which connect the main cities, and then the Expresos and Rápidos, which stop frequently. For a timetable ask for an *horario de trenes*; tourist information offices can also supply these.

RENFE Information:
www.renfe.es
(English translation available)
General enquiries Tel: 902 240 202
Seville Tel: 954 540 202
Córdoba Tel: 957 490 202
Granada Tel: 958 271 272

Right: taking to the open road

By Coach and Bus

Between Seville and Córdoba there's little to choose between train or coach, unless you are taking the AVE high-speed train, but for the longer journey to or from Granada the coach (3 hours) is more direct and arguably more scenic. Always take a coach if you are travelling between Málaga and Granada. One of the most useful companies is Alsina Graells, which operates an express service between Seville and Córdoba as well as other routes from these cities to Granada and Málaga (tel: Seville 95 441 8811; Córdoba 957 404040; Granada 958 185010).

If you are doing a lot of trips in Seville it is worth buying a *bonobus* 10-journey ticket or a *tarjeta turistica* (tourist pass), which is valid for 3 or 7 days. To visit the Itálica ruins take a bus to Santiponce.

In Seville buses for Córdoba or Granada leave from El Prado de San Sebastian, near the Parque de María Luisa . In Córdoba the bus station is at Plaza de las Tres Culturas, near the train station, and in Granada on Carretera de Jaén, quite a long way from the old city.

By Taxi

Taxis are a cheap and reliable way of getting around the three cities. A green *libre* sign indicates that a taxi is for hire. Fares are metered, but for long journeys or tours agree a price in advance.

Carriages

You will find these in Seville and to a lesser extent in Córdoba. They are expensive (agree a price and itinerary before setting out) but for many visitors an essential ingredient of their trip to Andalusia. In Seville,

Taxi Numbers
Seville Tel: 95 458 00 00/462 22 22
Córdoba Tel: 957 47 02 91
Granada Tel: 958 28 06 54

ACCOMMODATION

Hotels

The best hotels fill up quickly. If you're taking a short break you may prefer to book an all-inclusive flight and accommodation package before you leave, plus car hire if you require it. If you are touring, ring ahead to book a room – the hotel will probably ask you to arrive by a certain time, so ring again to let them know if you expect to be late. Some hotels, such as the Paradors or those close to the Alhambra, should be booked early. Hotels range from 1–5 star.

In the list of accommodation that follows, the approximate price for a double room with bath (including tax) are:

€€€€ More than €250
€€€ €150–250
€€ €100–150
€ Less than €100

IVA (Spanish VAT) of 7 percent is added to all hotel bills.

You may also encounter Hotel Residencias (HR) and Apartment Hotels where rooms have kitchen facilities. *Hostales*, graded 1–3 star, are small family-run hotels that vary from brilliant to dismal – ask to see the room first.

practical information

Other variations are the *Pensión* (P), *Fonda* (F) and *Casas de Huéspedes* (CH). Self-catering apartments (*apartamentos turisticos*) are best booked through an agent. The minimum stay for apartments is normally a week.

A detailed list of accommodation in each of these cities can be obtained in advance of your stay from the Spanish Tourist Office. Paradors (state-run luxury hotels) can be booked in the UK through Paradores de España (tel: 91 516 6666; www.parador.es).

Seville

Alfonso XIII
Calle San Fernando, 2
Tel: 954 917 000; Fax: 954 917 099
www.hotel-alfonsoxiii.com
Old-style elegance prevails in this classic Seville hotel, built in Neo-Mudéjar style during the late 1920s. The public rooms are magnificent, and the bedrooms sumptuous. Outdoor pool open in summer. Business centre. **€€€€**

Casa Imperial
Calle Imperial, 29
Tel: 954 500 300; Fax: 954 500 330
www.casaimperial.com
This stylish hostelry is in a restored 16th-century palace behind the Casa de Pilatos, with four inner patios. Some 24 suites, each decorated differently and with enormous bathrooms. Breakfast buffet included. **€€€**

Doña María
Calle Don Remondo 19
Tel: 954 224 990; Fax: 954 219 546
www.hdmaria.com
The location near the Giralda is a big plus at this old-fashioned hotel, but the service is below standard. Has a rooftop pool. **€€€**

Inglaterra
Plaza Nueva, 7
Tel: 954 224 970; Fax: 954 561 336
www.hotelinglaterra.es
Comfortable and friendly, overlooking the Plaza Nueva, a convenient location for touring the city. A British theme prevails in this long-established hotel, which includes the most authentic pub in Seville. **€€–€€€**

Los Seises
Calle Segovias, 6
Tel: 954 229 495; Fax: 954 224 334
www.hotellosseises.com
A unique location in a part of the 16th-century archbishop's Palace, beautifully restored and strikingly decorated to blend old elements with modern design. Rooftop pool with great view of the Giralda. **€€–€€€€**

Tryp Macarena
Calle San Juan de Ribera, 2
Tel: 954 375 800; Fax: 944 381 803
www.solmelia.com
An elegant, old-style exterior conceals a modern, comfortable hotel, across from the regional parliament and near the Macarena basilica. With over 300 rooms, it's a favourite with visiting businessmen. **€€–€€€**

Casa No 7
Calle Virgenes 7
Tel: 954 221 581; Fax: 954 214527
www.casanumero7.com
Small hotel in a 19th-century townhouse with individually decorated rooms. The emphasis is on comfort and good service. **€€€**

Las Casas de la Judería
Callejón de las Dos Hermanas
Tel: 954 415 150; Fax: 954 422 170
www.intergrouphoteles.com
This maze-like hotel converted from three old palaces in the Santa Cruz quarter is one of the most charming places to stay in Seville. Look out for special offers in low season. **€€**

Las Casas de los Mercaderes
Calle Alvarez Quintero 9-13
Tel: 954 225 858; Fax: 954 229 884
www.intergrouphoteles.com
Centred on a lovely 18th-century patio, this friendly, professionally run hotel located close to Seville's main sights is one of the best in its category, combining a charming setting with modern comfort. **€€**

Left: vying for visitors' attention

San Gil

Calle Parras, 28
Tel: 954 906 811; Fax: 954 906 939
www.sevillahotelsangil.com
Around the corner from the Macarena basilica, with spacious, modern rooms centred on a traditional patio. Its high standards make up for the fact that it is some distance from the main sights. Small roof-top pool. €€

Europa

Calle Jimios, 5
Tel: 954 500 443; Fax: 954 210 016
www.hoteleuropasevilla.com
A pleasant hotel in the budget category, with a cool Andalusian style inner courtyard, offering basic but clean lodgings. €

Hostal Goya

Calle Mateos Gago 31
Tel: 954 211 170; Fax: 954 562 988
www.hostalgoyasevilla.com
Antiquated but much-loved budget option in the Barrio Santa Cruz. €

Puerta de Triana

Calle Reyes Católicos, 5
Tel: 954 215 404; Fax: 954 215 401
www.hotelpuertadetriana.com
Friendly, efficient place, with small, adequate rooms. Good position near the river and within walking distance of the main sights. €

Hostería del Laurel

Plaza de los Venerables, 5
Tel: 954 220 295 ; Fax: 954 210 450
www.hosteriadellaurel.com
With its great location in the Barrio de Santa Cruz, this small hotel and restaurant is very popular. Basic but clean decor. €

Hotel Patio de la Cartuja

Calle Lumbreras, 8–10
Tel: 4 954 900 200; Fax: 954 902 056
www.patiosdesevilla.com
Set in a restored 'Corral de Vecinos' (home shared by several families). Modern rooms, some with kitchenettes. Next to the Alameda de Hércules, with its lively nightlife. €

Simon

Calle García de Vinuesa 19
Tel: 954 226 660; Fax: 954 562 241
www.hotelsimonsevilla.com
One of the best-value choices in the centre of Seville, not far from the cathedral, offering no-frills lodgings in an 18th-century house around an Andalusian patio. €

Zaida

Calle San Roque, 26
Tel: 954 211 138; Fax: 954 218 810
www.hotelzaida.com
This intimate budget hotel occupies a charming 18th-century town house with an attractive Mudejar-style courtyard. €

Córdoba

Conquistador

Calle Magistral González Francés, 15–17
Tel: 957 481 102; Fax: 957 474 677
www.hotelconquistadorcordoba.com
A long-established hotel next to the mosque. Rooms are large and modern, some have views of the mosque. €€€

Parador de Córdoba

Avenida de la Arruzafa
Tel: 957 275 900; Fax: 957 280 409
www.parador.es
Modern establishment situated on a hill on the outskirts of the city. Good views. €€

Al Mihrab

Avenida del Brillante, Km 5
Tel: 957 272 198; Fax: 957 272 198
This friendly, neo-Moorish style hotel is not far from the Parador, on the foothills north of central Córdoba. Great views. €€

Amistad Córdoba

Plaza de Maimónides, 3
Tel: 957 420 335; Fax: 957 420 365
www.nh-hotels.com
This is one of the best options in Córdoba if you want to be close to the sights. Comfortable, modern rooms in two former mansions looking over the Plaza Maimónides in the Judería. €€

Albucasis

Calle Buen Pastor, 11
Tel/Fax: 957 478 625

Family-run establishment offering good value for money and clean, comfortable lodgings around a central courtyard in the heart of the old town. €

Mezquita

Plaza Santa Catalina 1
Tel: 957 475 585; Fax: 957 476 219

Small hotel in a restored 16th-century palace. Superb location next to the mosque. €

Maestre

Calle Romero Barros 4–6
Tel: 957 472 410; Fax: 957 475 395
www.hotelmaestre.com

Near the historical Plaza del Potro, a small hotel offering inexpensive accommodation in rooms surrounding a cool inner patio. €

Granada

Alhambra Palace

Peña Partida, 2
Tel: 958 221 468; Fax: 958 226 404
www.h-alhambrapalace.es

Situated on the Alhambra hill, just outside the old walls, this ochre-coloured neo-Moorish fantasy has good views over the city. The hotel bar and terrace are a popular meeting place for locals and visitors alike. €€€

Melia Granada

Calle Angel Ganivet, 7
Tel: 958 227 400; Fax: 958 227 403
www.solmelia.com

Though not a particularly romantic option, this is a large, modern and efficient hotel located near to the post office, in the centre of the city. €€€

Parador de Granada

Alhambra
Tel: 958 221 440; Fax: 958 222 264
www.parador.es

Reservations are essential to get into the most sought-after rooms in this hotel belonging to the parador network. The hotel occupies a converted Franciscan monastery situated within the Alhambra gardens themselves. €€€

El Ladrón d'Agua

Carrera del Darro 13
Tel: 958 215 040; fax: 958 224 345
www.ladrondeagua.com

Beautifully restored 16th-century mansion with a lovely location alongside the Darro river. Very comfortable rooms, attractive patio and numerous period features. €€

Triunfo

Plaza Triunfo, 19
Tel: 958 207 444; Fax: 958 279 017

Above: Parador de Turismo de San Francisco

Just off Granada's main thoroughfare, the Gran Vía de Colón, and near the Cathedral. A small, comfortable hotel. €€

Zaguan del Darro
Carrera del Darro, 23
Tel: 958 215 730
Fax: 958 215 731
www.hotelzaguan.com
Like several other old mansions along the Carrera del Darro, it has been converted into charming and stylish hotel. Individually decorated, well-appointed rooms, some with a view of the Alhambra. Bar-coffee shop. €–€€

America
Real de la Alhambra, 53
Tel: 958 227 471; Fax: 958 227 470
www.hotelamericagranada.com
This is a small family-run hotel with an enviable location within the grounds of the Alhambra. Closed January and February. €–€€

Alixares
Avenida Alixares del Generalife
Tel: 958 225 575; Fax: 958 224 102
Modern hotel near the Alhambra. €€

Carmen de Santa Inés
San Juan de los Reyes, 15
Tel: 958 226380, Fax: 958 224404
www.carmensantaines.com
At the foot of Granada's Albaicín quarter, this small hotel occupies a converted 16th-century palace built around a traditional Andalusian courtyard. Rooms are individually furnished, and some have balconies. The unusual, labyrinthine layout of the hotel means that rooms vary considerably. €€

Reina Cristina
Calle Tablas, 4
Tel: 958 253 211; Fax: 958 255 728
www.hotelreinacristina.com
A friendly and comfortable establishment in an old Granada house, where Federico García Lorca spent his last days. Well-located midway between the cathedral and the Plaza Bib Rambla. Good restaurant. €€

Hostal Suecia
Huerta de los Angeles, 8
Tel: 958 225 044; Fax: 958 225 044
Hotel Suecia occupies an old villa at the foot of the Alhambra hill. A pleasant and informal family-run, budget place, it offers accommodation in 12 rooms surrounded by a pretty garden. €

Pension Doña Lupe
Avenida del Generalife
Tel: 958 221 473; Fax: 958 221 474
www.donalupegranada.com
Pension Doña Lupe is a good budget option for those looking for basic facilities but a great location – right next to the Alhambra. €

USEFUL INFORMATION

Tourist Offices

For information about Andalusia, contact www.andalucia.org.

Tourist offices in Spain are generally helpful but usually busy. All of them offer free maps and information; those run by the Junta de Andalusia (listed first below) also have leaflets. Every large city has a Municipal Tourist Office as well (listed second), which primarily dispenses local information. Offices are normally open 9am–7pm Mon–Sat and 10am–2pm Sun.

Seville Av de la Constitución 21, tel: 954 787 578; Costurero de la Reina, Paseo de la Delicias, tel: 95 423 44 65.

Córdoba Calle Torrijos 10 (Palacio de Congresos), tel: 957 47 12 35.

Granada Plaza Mariana Pineda 10, tel: 958 247 146; Corral del Carbón, tel: 958 22 59 90; www.turgranada.com

In **London** the Spanish National Tourist Office is at 22–23 Manchester Square, London W1M 5AP, tel: 020-7486 8077, fax: 020-7486 8034; email: info.londres@tourspain.es; www.tourspain.co.uk. Brochures and hotel listings can be ordered on the internet or by telephoning the premium-line number (also for information): tel: 084 59400180 (UK) or tel: 0818 220290 (Republic of Ireland).

In the **USA**, contact 666 Fifth Avenue 35th Floor New York 10103, tel: (212) 265 8822, fax: (212) 265 8864. Also branches in Chicago, Miami and Los Angeles. See www. okspain.org.

In **Canada**, contact 2 Bloor St West 34th Floor, Toronto, Ontarior M4W 3E2, tel: (416) 961 3131, fax: (416) 961 1992.

Tipping and Service

Tipping is usual but not obligatory – around 5–10 per cent for taxi-drivers and at least €1 for porters. Some restaurants will add a service charge, but many people leave an additional tip. In bars it will costs more if you sit down at a table and are served by a waiter than if you stand or perch at the bar.

Concessions

Senior citizens and students are often eligible for reduced admission charges, but will need to provide proof of status (passport in the case of senior citizens). EU citizens are given free entry to some museums.

Facilities for the Disabled

Andalusia is a viable destination for disabled travellers, but facilities vary considerably. The best are found in the resorts of the Costa del Sol. For additional information consult RADAR, tel: 020-7250 3222, fax: 020-7250 0212, www.radar.org.uk, who can provide general information on travelling abroad; or Holiday Care, tel: 01293-774535, fax: 01293-784647, www.holidaycare.org.uk, who publish useful information sheets on a number of destinations.

Children

The Spanish think children should be seen, heard and utterly spoilt. They're not just tolerated but enjoyed. Most hotels can provide cots and highchairs (book ahead) while baby food, nappies, powdered milk , etc are available in supermarkets. Babysitters can usually be arranged through hotels, or ask tourist offices about private services available locally, though even very young children will be welcome in restaurants during the evening.

Right: fun for the young

Hire-car firms can supply child seats but these should be ordered in advance (take a sun-screen for the windows). It is against the law for children under 12 to travel in the front seat. On RENFE children under four travel free, and under 12 half-price.

Specific attractions for children include Isla Mágica *(see page 36)*, a theme park built around the artificial lake created for Expo '92 on the Isla Cartuja. It has a good range of roller-coasters and other white-knuckle attractions, plus tamer rides for small children.

Consulates
United Kingdom
Calle Mauricio Moro Pareto 2-2º, Málaga
Tel: 95 235 23 00
USA
Paseo de la Delicias 7, Seville
Tel: 95 423 18 85

MEDIA & COMMUNICATIONS

In Seville newspapers such as *El Correo* and *ABC* publish listings of forthcoming cultural events in the city. In addition, a what's on magazine entitled *El Giraldillo* is published weekly and available free from Tourist Offices, museums and cultural venues. In Córdoba the daily paper *Córdoba* has a section of useful information including late-night chemists and train and bus timetables, as does *Ideal* in Granada.

Telephones

Telephone boxes are found on almost every street corner and accept both coins and phone cards *(tarjetas telefónicas)*, which can be bought in various denominations from news and tobacco kiosks. Calls can also be made from multi-boothed *cabinas* in the city centre where you pay an assistant afterwards. These are useful for long-distance calls.

Main Telephone Offices:
Seville: Plaza Nueva 3
Córdoba: Plaza de las Tendillas
Granada: Calle Reyes Católicos

To call other countries, dial the international access code 00, then the country code: Australia (61); France (33); Germany (49); Italy (39); Japan (81); Netherlands (31); UK (44); US and Canada (1). Calls cost less between 10pm and 8am.

Phone Access Codes

Direct Enquiries 1003
British Telecom 900 990 044
ATT 900 990 011
MCI 900 990 014
Sprint 900 990 013

INTERNET

Seville, Granada and Córdoba have many cyber cafés and Internet bureaus, where you can check up on your email. Rates are around €1.80–3 per hour. Most of the better hotels also offer internet facilities, but check before booking if this is important to you.

BUSINESS HOURS

Spanish hours are vulnerable to what happened the night before, but you will find the majority of businesses in action by around 9am. Activity then stops at 1 or 1.30pm – for the Spanish day is traditionally divided by a long lunch followed by a siesta, a practice well worth observing, especially in summer. Business resumes again about 4.30pm (5pm in summer) and continues until about 7 or 8pm. Government offices often start at 8am and work through until 3pm.

Banks are more punctual, and open 9am–2pm Monday to Friday. They are also open for business on Saturdays 9am–1pm from October to April. As in the UK, many transactions can also be done at *cajas de ahorros* (savings banks) which sometimes keep longer hours. Money can be changed *(cambio)* at hotels, and bureaux de change travel agents.

Post Offices *(Oficinas de Correos)* open at least 9am–1pm Monday to Saturday, with main ones open all day. Stamps *(sellos)* can be bought in tobacconists (called *estancos*, but look for a brown and yellow 'T' sign saying '*tabacos*'). They can also be bought at most hotel receptions.

Main Post Offices (for Poste Restante – *Lista de Correos* – mail):
Seville: Avenida de la Constitución 32, tel: 95 421 95 85.
Córdoba: Calle Cruz Conde 21, tel: 957 478 267.
Granada: Puerta Real 1, tel: 958 22 11 38.

HEALTH & EMERGENCIES

Beware the sun's strength. It is extremely easy to get burnt, even up in the cooler mountains. Use a high-protection-factor suntan cream, wear a sunhat and always take a bottle of water with you. Stay in the shade during the hottest part of the day.

Left: catching up on the news

For minor health problems chemists *(farmacias)* are a good source of advice; staff often speak English. They are devoted solely to dispensing medication and are marked by a green cross. Numerous medicines only available by prescription in the UK are available over the counter in Spain, which can be handy if you leave a vital medication at home, though obviously you will need to know its name and dosage.

Don't confuse *farmacias* with *droguerías*, which only sell perfume and toiletries. *Farmacias* have a rota of after-hours service *(farmacia de guardia)*: to find this look for a sign posted in the window or in the local paper. For a doctor *(médico)* or dentist *(dentista),* ask at your hotel or in the Tourist Information Office.

Emergency Telephone Numbers
Police and Emergency: *(urgencia)* 091
Fire Brigade: 080
Medical emergency: 061
Seville: 954 222 222
Córdoba: 957 293 411
Granada: 958 28 20 00

Police
Policemen come in three different-coloured uniforms. In urban areas the *Policía Nacional* (dark-blue uniforms) rule the streets while the *Policía Municipal* (blue uniforms with a white band on their caps) control the traffic. The *Guardia Civil* (olive-green uniforms) rule everything else. Despite the sunglasses and swaggers, they're generally all quite helpful.

Should anything unfortunate happen to you, tell your hotel receptionist or your holiday representative, who should then help you inform the Policía Nacional and make a statement, a copy of which should be supplied for insurance purposes.

Main police stations are:
Seville: Plaza de la Gavidia,
tel: 954 289 300.
Córdoba: Avenida del Dr Fleming 2,
tel: 957 47 75 00.
Granada: Plaza de los Campos,
tel: 958 28 21 50.

Toilets
There are very few public toilets, so the best option is to pop into a bar, hotel or restaurant and use the *servicios* (sometimes *aseos*) – it is polite to ask permission first and usual to leave a small tip if there is an attendant.

FURTHER READING

Other Guide Books
Insight Regional Guide: Southern Spain (Apa Publications, 2007) offers up-to-date information, in-depth essays on Andalusia and the Costa del Sol, and a pullout map.

Insight Pocket Guide: Costa del Sol (Apa Publications, 2007). Tailor-made itineraries linking the best of the coast, plus a large pull-out map.

Cultural/Background
Alistair Boyd's *The Road to Ronda* (Collins) and **Penelope Chetwode**'s *Two Middle-Aged Ladies in Andalusia* (Century) describe horse-riding trips in the 1960s.

Gerald Brenan's *South from Granada* (Cambridge) describes his life in the Alpujarras in the 1920s.

Miguel de Cervantes' *Exemplary Novels* are cautionary tales from 17th-century Spain and a good warm-up prior to tackling *Don Quixote* (both Penguin Classics).

Poems of Arab Andalusia translated by **Cola Franzen** (City Lights Books) will transport you straight back to the world of al-Andalus.

Ian Gibson's *Federico García Lorca* (Faber) is a biography of Spain's greatest modern poet.

Washington Irving's *Tales of the Alhambra* is essential Granada reading.

Nicholas Luard's *Andalucía* (Century) and **Hugh Seymour-Davies'** *The Bottlebrush Tree* (Constable) tell of life in an Andalusian village.

Driving Over Lemons: An Optimist in Spain, by **Chris Stewart**, relating the author's experience of living and working in a remote valley of the Alpujarras, proved an international bestseller in the late 1990s.

ACKNOWLEDGEMENTS

8/9	**Stuart Abraham**
58T, 68	**Junta de Andalucia**
36	**J.D. Dallet**
1, 20, 21, 23, 24T/B, 52, 55, 56, 57, 61, 65, 67, 72, 80, 81, 83, 84, 87, 89, 90	**Jerry Dennis**
11, 13, 32B	**Andrew Eames**
37, 39	**H. Herbeisen/Marco Polo**
64	**Nick Inman**
16, 28, 44T, 46	**Lyle Lawson**
38	**Hidalgo Lopesino/Marco Polo**
10	**José Martin**
34, 35	**Don Murray**
23	**Alice Prier**
27, 29, 32T, 33, 40, 43, 44B, 47, 48T/B, 49, 50, 51, 60, 66, 69, 77, 78	**Mark Read**
63	**Capilla Real**
14, 15, 41, 53, 58B, 63B, 71, 75	**Nigel Tisdall**
30	**Gregory Wrona**
Cover	**Doug Scott/age fotostock/Powerstock**
Cartography	**Maria Donnelly/Apa Publications**

© Apa Publications GmbH & Co. Verlag KG Singapore Branch, Singapore

INDEX

index **95**

festivals and events 78–9
flamenco 74
Franco 16

Getting around 83–4
getting there 82
González, Felipe 16
Granada 13, 15, 53–63
  accommodation 87–8
  Albaicín 60–62
  Alhambra 13, 15, 53–60
    Alcazaba 54
    Charles V Palace 55
    Generalife 59–60
    Jardín de los Adarves 56
    Museo Bellas Artes 55
    Museo de la Alhambra 55
    Nasrid Palaces 59
  Alhambra Palace Hotel 60
  Capilla Real 63
  Casa Manuel de Falla museum 60
  Cathedral 63
  Corral del Carbón 63
  eating out 73
  El Bañuelo 62
  Madraza University, La 63
  Mirador de San Cristóbal 60
  Monasterio Santa Isabel la Real 61
  Museo Arqueológico 62
  Parador de San Francisco 54
  Paseo del Padre Manjón 62
  Plaza de Bib-Rambla 62
  Plaza Isabel la Católica 63
  Plaza Larga 61
  Plaza Nueva 60
  Plaza Padre Suarez 63
  Plaza San Miguel Bajo 61
  Puerta Nueva 61
  shopping 68
Guadalquivir River 11, 15, 16, 30, 38, 45

Health and emergencies 81, 90–91
Hemingway, Ernest 16
history & culture 11–17

Ibero-American Exposition of 1929 16, 21, 28
Ibn-al-Ahmar 13, 54
Inquisition 13, 14

Irving, Washington 15, 59
Itálica 11

Jewish community of Córdoba 46–7
Juan Carlos 16

Lanjarón 65
La Rábida monastery 39
Lorca, Federico García 16
Lucena 51

Mañara, Don Miguel de 30
Marismas, Las 11
Medinat Al-Zahra 12, 49
Montilla 50
Moors 11–13, 42, 46, 53–4, 65
moriscos 14, 60
Muelle de las Carabelas 39
Mulhacen 64
Murillo, Bartolomé Esteban 14

Niebla 39
nightlife 74–6

Órgiva 65

Palacio de Acebrón 38
Palos de la Frontera 39
Pampaneira 65
Pedro the Cruel 13, 26
Peninsular War 15
Pradollano 64
Priego de Córdoba 51
Primo de Rivera, Miguel 15–16

Rábida monastery, La 12
Reconquest 13, 23, 26
Roman occupation 11

Sanlúcar de Barrameda 11, 12
Santa María de las Cueva monastery 12
Seville 11, 15
  accommodation 85–6
  Archivo General de Indias 14, 29
  Auditorio de La Cartuja 36
  Ayuntamiento 33
  Barrio Santa Cruz 31
  Basilica de la Macarena 35
  Calle San Andrés 34